MOVIE ★ ICONS

NICHOLSON

EDITOR
PAUL DUNCAN

TEXT
DOUGLAS KEESEY

PHOTOS
THE KOBAL COLLECTION

TASCHEN

HONG KONG KÖLN LONDON LOS ANGELES MADRID PARIS TOKYO

CONTENTS

1

JACK NICHOLSON: WILD MAN

BY DOUGLAS KEESEY

JACK NICHOLSON: DER WILDE MANN

JACK NICHOLSON: LE SAUVAGE

JACK NICHOLSON: WILD MAN

by Douglas Keesey

At the 1993 Academy Awards, the host said "Jack" and millions of viewers knew exactly who was about to appear. He has been nominated 12 times for an Oscar (at least once in every decade since the 1960s), and has won three times. Jack is also a perennial fixture in the front row at the Oscar ceremonies, flashing his devilish grin, arching his eyebrows, and wearing his trademark indoor sunglasses. As Billy Crystal joked, "Nicholson has to wear sunglasses 'cause he gets in his own reflection, his aura is so great."

But Jack was not always Jack. First he paid his dues in Hollywood, taking small TV parts and working in low-budget teen, biker, horror, and adventure films for 11 years. Although he was lucky enough to land the lead role in his movie debut, *The Cry Baby Killer* (1958), the film was relegated to second-bill drive-in fare and Jack returned to obscurity. However, some of Jack's early works have since achieved cult status—for instance, *The Little Shop of Horrors* (1960), in which he played a pain-loving dental patient ("No novocaine—it dulls the senses!"), and *The Shooting* (1966), an existentialist western with Jack as a sneering gunslinger garbed in black.

Ironically, Jack was over 30 when the youth movie *Easy Rider* (1969) finally made him a star. In the role of an alcoholic Southern lawyer who joins up with bikers played by Peter Fonda and Dennis Hopper on a drug-fueled trip across America, Jack cemented his image as an antiestablishment outlaw, a free-spirited individualist always bucking the system. His reputation as a rebellious antihero was furthered by three notorious confrontations in films of the 1970s. First, a rule-bound waitress provoked him to clear a café table with one sweep of his arm in *Five Easy Pieces* (1970). Then, in *The Last Detail* (1973), a surly bartender caused him to explode in a gun-brandishing fury. And finally, *One Flew Over the Cuckoo's Nest* (1975) had Jack leading the inmates of an insane asylum to riot for their freedom against the repressive Nurse Ratched. As Jack has said about these

STILL FROM 'THE CROSSING GUARD' (1995)

"What is stardom for if you don't take chances?"
Jack Nicholson

moments when his characters erupt in anger, "I jump from immaculately polite to violent—there's not much rudeness in between. Rudeness is for amateurs." But rebellious youth have no monopoly on violence, and in later years Jack has also played sadistic father figures: the ax-wielding Jack Torrance in *The Shining* (1980), the gleefully psychotic Joker in *Batman* (1989), a hotheaded marine colonel in *A Few Good Men* (1992), and a ruthless mob boss up to his elbows in blood in *The Departed* (2006). Jack's over-the-top performances in these larger-than-life roles have led some to criticize him for hammy acting and cartoon villainy, but they have also fed his iconic image as "The Wild Man of Hollywood."

Perhaps surprisingly, given that he does not have matinee-idol good looks, Jack is also renowned for being "The Great Seducer" and the unlikely star of a whole series of sexually charged melodramas and romantic comedies. "He lost his hair, grew a gut, and yet became more of a sex symbol than ever," Erik Lundegaard has noted. Whether he is making passionate love on the kitchen table with Jessica Lange in *The Postman Always Rings Twice* (1981) or frolicking fully clothed in the ocean waves with Shirley MacLaine in *Terms of Endearment* (1983), Jack is a seductive devil. In fact, he played the Devil in *The Witches of Eastwick* (1987), seducing three desperate housewives.

As true fans of Jack know, some of his best performances are in less showy roles where his power is conveyed through the subtlety of his acting. Jack has often turned down parts in big moneymakers (*The Godfather*, *The Sting*, *Wall Street*, *Space Cowboys*) in order to take riskier roles such as the introverted and grimly brooding men in *Ironweed* (1987), *The Crossing Guard* (1995), *The Pledge* (2001), and *About Schmidt* (2002). Jack—The Wild Man, The Great Seducer—is also a very fine actor indeed, and in *Chinatown* (1974) he gives what may be his most memorable performance as private eye Jake Gittes, wisecracking but vulnerable, supremely self-confident despite the bandage across his nose.

JACK NICHOLSON: DER WILDE MANN

von Douglas Keesey

Bei der Oscar-Verleihung 1993 kündigte der Moderator nur „Jack" an, und Millionen von Zuschauern wussten haargenau, wer auf die Bühne treten würde. Er wurde zwölf Mal für einen Academy Award nominiert (mindestens ein Mal in jedem Jahrzehnt seit den 1960er-Jahren) und wurde drei Mal damit ausgezeichnet. Jack gehört bei dieser Veranstaltung zum Inventar, wenn er mit seinem teuflischen Grinsen in der ersten Reihe sitzt, seine Augenbrauen hebt und natürlich sein Markenzeichen, die unverkennbare Sonnenbrille, trägt, über die Billy Crystal scherzte: „Nicholson muss eine Sonnenbrille tragen, damit er nicht von seiner eigenen Aura geblendet wird."

Aber Jack war nicht immer Jack. Er arbeitete sich in Hollywood Schritt für Schritt nach oben, indem er zunächst kleine Fernsehrollen annahm und elf Jahre lang in billigen Teenie-, Biker-, Horror- und Abenteuerstreifen mitwirkte. Wenngleich er das Glück hatte, in seinem Debütfilm *The Cry Baby Killer* (1958) gleich die Hauptrolle zu ergattern, war es ein Film, der bloß im Nebenprogramm der Autokinos lief, und Jack verschwand rasch wieder in der Versenkung. Dennoch haben einige von Jacks frühen Werken inzwischen Kultstatus erlangt – zum Beispiel sein kurzer Auftritt als masochistischer Zahnarztpatient („Kein Novocain – es stumpft die Sinne ab!") in *Kleiner Laden voller Schrecken* (1960) oder *Das Schießen* (1966), ein existenzialistischer Western mit Jack in der Rolle eines höhnischen, schwarz gekleideten Revolverhelden.

Ironischerweise war Jack schon über 30, als ihn der Jugendfilm *Easy Rider* (1969) schließlich zum Star machte. Als alkoholkranker Rechtsanwalt aus den Südstaaten, der sich den von Peter Fonda und Dennis Hopper gespielten Motorradfahrern auf ihrem Drogentrip quer durch die USA anschließt, zementierte Jack sein Image als gesetzloser Kämpfer gegen das Establishment, als freigeistiger Individualist, der sich stets gegen das System auflehnt. Seinen Ruf als aufsässiger Antiheld festigte er weiter durch drei berühmt-berüchtigte Konfrontationsszenen in Filmen der 1970er-Jahre. Zunächst provozierte ihn in *Ein Mann sucht sich selbst* (1970) eine Bedienung, die sich streng an ihre Vorschriften hielt, bis er mit einer einzigen Armbewegung den Tisch eines Cafés

STILL FROM 'THE BORDER' (1982)

„Was ist Starruhm, wenn man kein Risiko eingeht?"
Jack Nicholson

abräumte. Dann brachte ihn ein mürrischer Barmann in *Das letzte Kommando* (1973) zur Weißglut, bis die Szene in einer wilden Schießerei endete. Und schließlich stiftete Jack in *Einer flog über das Kuckucksnest* (1975) die Insassen einer Irrenanstalt an, gegen die unterdrückerische Schwester Ratched um ihre Freiheit zu kämpfen. Jack erklärte diese Wutausbrüche seiner Figuren so: „Ich springe sofort von tadelloser Höflichkeit zur Gewalttätigkeit – dazwischen gibt es nicht viele Unverschämtheiten. Unverschämtheit ist für Anfänger." Aber Gewalt ist kein Monopol aufsässiger Jugendlicher, und so spielte Jack in späteren Jahren auch sadistische Vaterfiguren: den axtschwingenden Jack Torrance in *Shining* (1980), den schadenfroh psychotischen Joker in *Batman* (1989), einen hitzköpfigen Obristen in *Eine Frage der Ehre* (1992) und einen skrupellosen Mafiaboss, der bis zu den Ellbogen im Blut steckt, in *Departed: Unter Feinden* (2006). Manche kritisierten Jack für seine überzogene Darstellung dieser überlebensgroßen Figuren als durchgeknallten Cartoon-Bösewicht, aber diese Rollen halfen ihm auch, sein Image als „der wilde Mann von Hollywood" weiter auszubauen.

Es mag überraschen, dass Jack, der nicht über das gute Aussehen manch eines Frauenschwarms verfügt, auch als „großer Verführer" gilt und Hauptrollen in einer ganzen Reihe sexuell geladener Melodramen und Liebeskomödien spielte. „Er hat seine Haare verloren, einen Bauch bekommen und ist doch mehr Sexsymbol als je zuvor", bemerkte Erik Lundegaard. Ob er Jessica Lange in *Wenn der Postmann zweimal klingelt* (1981) leidenschaftlich auf dem Küchentisch liebt oder sich voll bekleidet mit Shirley MacLaine in *Zeit der Zärtlichkeit* (1983) in den Wellen tummelt: Jack ist ein verführerischer Teufel. Und tatsächlich spielte er in *Die Hexen von Eastwick* (1987) den Teufel höchstpersönlich, der drei verzweifelte Hausfrauen verführt.

Wie Jacks wahre Fans wissen, lieferte er aber einige seiner besten Leistungen in weniger spektakulären Rollen, in denen er sein Talent eher im unterschwelligen Spiel bewies. Jack hat oft Rollen in großen kommerziellen Produktionen (*Der Pate*, *Der Clou*, *Wall Street*, *Space Cowboys*) abgelehnt, um riskantere Typen zu spielen, wie etwa die grimmig-grüblerischen, introvertierten Figuren in *Wolfsmilch* (1987), *The Crossing Guard* (1995), *Das Versprechen* (2001) und *About Schmidt* (2002). Jack – der Wilde, der große Verführer – ist tatsächlich auch ein sehr guter Schauspieler, und in *Chinatown* (1974) liefert er seine möglicherweise denkwürdigste darstellerische Leistung als Privatdetektiv Jake Gittes, stets einen Scherz auf den Lippen und doch verwundbar und außerordentlich selbstbewusst trotz des Pflasters auf der Nase.

STILL FROM 'IRONWEED' (1987)
As alcoholic ex-baseball star Francis Phelan—a role Jack modeled on his own grandfather. / Als alkoholsüchtiger ehemaliger Baseballstar Francis Phelan – eine Rolle, die Nicholson seinem eigenen Großvater nachempfand. / Pour le rôle de Francis Phelan, ancienne star du base-ball devenue alcoolique, Nicholson s'inspire de son grand-père.

JACK NICHOLSON: LE SAUVAGE

Douglas Keesey

En 1993, lorsque le présentateur de la cérémonie des Oscars annonce « Jack », des millions de spectateurs, dans la salle et derrière leurs téléviseurs, savent exactement qui va apparaître sur scène. Nominé douze fois par le jury des Academy Awards – au moins une fois par décennie depuis les années 1960 –, Jack Nicholson a remporté trois oscars. Il est un habitué si fidèle du premier rang de cette cérémonie que son faciès diabolique, ses sourcils arqués et ses lunettes noires semblent faire partie du décor. Comme le dit Billy Crystal ce soir-là avec beaucoup d'humour, « Nicholson est obligé de toujours porter des lunettes de soleil parce qu'il perçoit son propre reflet et son aura est si lumineuse qu'elle l'éblouit ».

Mais « Jack » n'a pas toujours été « Jack », et le chemin de Hollywood fut long et laborieux. Pendant onze ans, il accepte des petits rôles à la télévision, dans des films à petit budget pour adolescents ou pour motards, des films d'horreur ou d'aventure. Il a la chance d'obtenir le rôle principal dans son premier film, *The Cry Baby Killer* (1958), mais le film n'est projeté que dans des drive-in de seconde zone, et Nicholson retourne à l'anonymat. Certains de ses films précoces deviendront cependant cultes, comme *La Petite Boutique des horreurs* (1960), dans lequel il joue le patient masochiste d'un dentiste (« Pas de novocaïne... ça atténue les sensations ! ») ou *The Shooting* (1966), un western existentialiste où Nicholson campe le personnage d'un as de la gâchette railleur vêtu de noir.

Étrangement, Nicholson a dépassé la trentaine quand le film pour adolescents *Easy Rider* (1969) fait de lui une star. Dans le rôle d'un avocat alcoolique du Sud qui se joint à deux motards (Peter Fonda et Dennis Hopper) pour un voyage rythmé par la drogue à travers les États-Unis, Nicholson scelle son image de hors-la-loi marginal, de libre-penseur individualiste aux prises avec le système. Sa réputation d'antihéros rebelle sera servie par trois autres rôles forts dans les années 1970 – trois moments d'intense confrontation. D'abord dans *Cinq pièces faciles* (1970) où, face à une serveuse revêche et butée, il nettoie une table de dîner d'un efficace revers de bras. Ensuite dans *La Dernière Corvée* (1973), où, poussé à bout par un barman rébarbatif, il déclenche une fusillade furieuse. Enfin dans *Vol au-dessus d'un nid de coucou* (1975), dans lequel il pousse les patients d'un asile d'aliénés à se révolter et à se libérer de l'emprise de l'infirmière Ratched. Nicholson commentera ainsi ces moments où ses personnages laissent libre cours à leur rage : « Je saute de la politesse immaculée à la violence – entre les deux, il n'y a pas de place pour l'insolence. L'insolence, c'est pour les amateurs. » Mais la jeunesse rebelle n'a pas le monopole de la violence et Nicholson jouera également des figures paternelles sadiques les années suivantes : le manieur de hache Jack Torrance de *Shining* (1980), le Joker allègrement psychotique de *Batman* (1989), un impétueux colonel de la marine dans *Des hommes d'honneur* (1992) et un caïd de la pègre avec du sang jusqu'aux coudes dans *Les Infiltrés* (2006). Dans chacun de ces rôles d'une rare densité, la performance exceptionnelle de Nicholson provoque la critique de certains, qui la juge trop caricaturale, à la limite du grotesque ; c'est pourtant bien elle qui nourrira son image mythique de « sauvage » de Hollywood.

On pourrait s'étonner que Nicholson, qui n'a ni le physique d'un jeune premier, ni celui du gendre idéal, soit aussi connu comme le « grand séducteur de ses dames », héros improbable d'une série de mélodrames et de comédies romantiques à forte charge sexuelle. « Il a perdu ses cheveux, pris du ventre, et pourtant, il est plus que jamais un sex-symbol », remarque Erik Lundegaard. Qu'il fasse fiévreusement l'amour à Jessica Lange sur la table de la cuisine dans *Le facteur sonne toujours deux fois* (1981) ou qu'il batifole dans les vagues, entièrement vêtu, avec Shirley MacLaine dans *Tendres passions* (1983), Nicholson reste un séducteur redoutable. Il jouera d'ailleurs le Diable en personne, corrupteur de trois femmes au foyer désespérées, dans *Les Sorcières d'Eastwick* (1987).

Comme le savent les vrais admirateurs de Nicholson, il excelle surtout dans des rôles moins tapageurs, où il communique sa puissance par la subtilité du jeu. Nicholson a souvent refusé des rôles dans des films très lucratifs et populaires (*Le Parrain*, *L'Arnaque*, *Wall Street*, *Space Cowboys*) pour endosser des rôles plus risqués, comme ceux de personnages maussades, introvertis et en quête de sens dans *La Force du destin* (1987), *Crossing Guard* (1995), *The Pledge* (2001) et *Monsieur Schmidt* (2002). Jack le « sauvage » et le « grand séducteur » est aussi un très grand acteur et dans *Chinatown* (1974), il donne toute la mesure de son talent pour incarner le détective privé Jake Gittes, acerbe mais vulnérable, d'une assurance absolue malgré le bandage qui lui barre le nez.

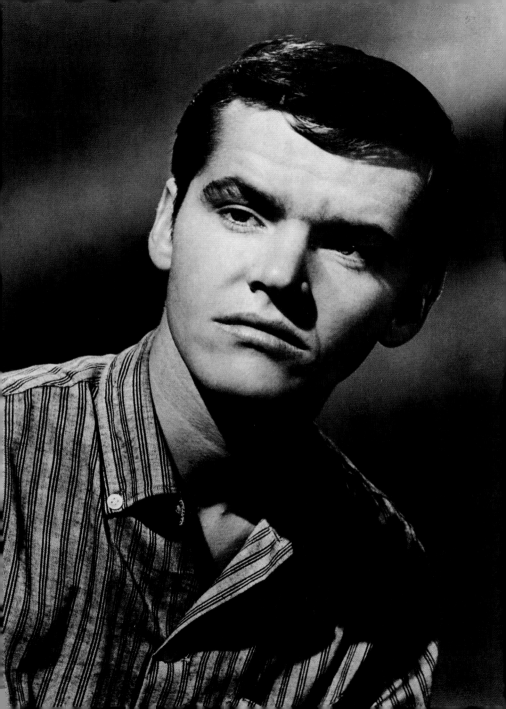

2

VISUAL FILMOGRAPHY

FILMOGRAFIE IN BILDERN

FILMOGRAPHIE EN IMAGES

YESTERDAY a Teenage Rebel...
TODAY a mad-dog slayer!

CRY BABY KILLER

Starring
HARRY LAUTER · JACK NICHOLSON · CAROLYN MITCHELL

Executive Producer ROGER CORMAN
Produced by DAVID KRAMARSKY and DAVID MARCH
Directed by JUS ADDISS · Screenplay by LEO GORDON
and MELVIN LEVY · An ALLIED ARTISTS Picture

HEAR Dick Kallman sing "CRY BABY CRY"

POSTER FOR 'THE CRY BABY KILLER' (1958)
Jack's movie debut—and in the lead role! But the film
went largely unnoticed. / Nicholsons Filmdebüt – und
das gleich in der Hauptrolle! Leider lief der Film
weitgehend unbemerkt. / La première apparition de
Nicholson au cinéma – et dans le premier rôle! Mais le
film passe quasiment inaperçu.

*"For years, I either played the clean-cut boy next
door or the murderer of a family of five."*
Jack Nicholson on his early film roles

*„Jahrelang spielte ich entweder den Saubermann
von nebenan oder den Mörder einer fünfköpfigen
Familie."*
Jack Nicholson über seine frühen Filmrollen

*« Pendant des années, j'ai joué soit le gendre idéal,
soit le meurtrier d'une famille nombreuse. »*
Jack Nicholson à propos de ses débuts

STILL FROM 'THE CRY BABY KILLER' (1958)
A sensitive youth brutally beaten and turned into a
juvenile delinquent. / Ein sensibler junger Mann wird
brutal zusammengeschlagen und dadurch zum
jugendlichen Straftäter. / Un jeune homme à l'âme
sensible est battu avec brutalité et sombre dans la
délinquance juvénile.

STILL FROM 'STUDS LONIGAN' (1960)
Jack plays a street tough who rapes a young woman at a
gin party. Based on the James T. Farrell novel trilogy. /
Nicholson spielt einen Schläger von der Straße, der bei
einer Gin-Party eine junge Frau vergewaltigt. Nach der
Romantrilogie von James T. Farrell. / Nicholson joue un
voyou qui viole une jeune femme au cours d'une soirée
arrosée. Adaptation de la trilogie de James T. Farrell.

"Unpredictability is the most arresting quality an actor can have."
Jack Nicholson

„Unberechenbarkeit ist die umwerfendste Eigenschaft, die ein Schauspieler besitzen kann."
Jack Nicholson

« L'imprévisibilité est la qualité la plus saisissante que puisse avoir un acteur. »
Jack Nicholson

STILL FROM 'THE RAVEN' (1963)
As the romantic lead in this comedy-horror film with Peter Lorre, Vincent Price, and Hazel Court. / Als herzensbrechende Hauptfigur in einer Horrorkomödie mit Peter Lorre, Vincent Price und Hazel Court. / Un rôle de jeune premier dans cette comédie d'horreur avec Peter Lorre, Vincent Price et Hazel Court.

STILL FROM 'THE RAVEN' (1963)
Producer-director Roger Corman's low-budget films
could at least boast a fiery finale. / Wenigstens hatten
die Billigfilme des Produzenten und Regisseurs Roger
Corman ein spektakuläres Finale. / Dans les films à petit
budget du producteur et réalisateur Roger Corman,
la scène finale est toujours flamboyante.

PAGES 30/31
STILL FROM 'THE TERROR'' (1963)
André Duvalier (Nicholson) falls in love with the
mysterious Helene (Sandra Knight—Jack's real-life wife
at the time). / André Duvalier (Nicholson) verliebt sich
in die rätselhafte Hélène (Sandra Knight, die zum
damaligen Zeitpunkt mit Nicholson verheiratet war). /
André Duvalier (Nicholson) tombe amoureux de la
mystérieuse Hélène (Sandra Knight, alors l'épouse de
Nicholson dans la vie).

STILL FROM 'THE TERROR' (1963)
The Raven and The Terror were made back to back,
with the latter filmed in four days using the same sets. /
Der Rabe: Duell der Zauberer und Schloss des
Schreckens wurden hintereinander in den gleichen
Kulissen abgedreht – Letzterer in vier Drehtagen. /
Les tournages du Corbeau et de L'Halluciné
s'enchaînent : le second a été achevé en quatre jours
et utilise les mêmes décors que le premier.

STILL FROM 'THE TERROR' (1963)
Trying to pry the secret from Baron Von Leppe, played
by horror-film legend Boris Karloff. / Hier versucht
André, das Geheimnis des Barons von Leppe in Erfah-
rung zu bringen, der von Horrorfilmlegende Boris
Karloff gespielt wird. / Tentant d'arracher son secret au
baron von Leppe, joué par la légende du film d'horreur
Boris Karloff.

"There are two ways up the ladder,
hand over hand or scratching and clawing.
It's sure been tough on my nails."
Jack Nicholson on his early years in Hollywood

„Es gibt zwei Möglichkeiten, die Leiter
hinaufzuklettern: eine Hand über die andere
oder durch Kratzen und Schlagen. Es war gewiss
hart für meine Nägel."
Jack Nicholson über seine frühen Jahre in Hollywood

STILL FROM 'BACK DOOR TO HELL' (1964)
In a war drama with costar and friend John Hackett,
who would later double as Jack's stand-in on
subsequent films. / In einem Kriegsdrama mit seinem
Kollegen und Freund John Hackett, der in späteren
Filmen auch Nicholsons Lichtdouble war. / Dans un film
de guerre dramatique aux côtés de son ami John
Hackett, qui servira ensuite de doublure à Nicholson
dans ses prochains films.

« Il y a deux manières de grimper l'échelle :
soit en posant les mains l'une après l'autre,
soit en s'y agrippant de toutes ses griffes.
Et c'est sûr, mes ongles ont souffert. »
Jack Nicholson à propos de ses premières années
à Hollywood

JACK NICHOLSON

RIDE IN THE WHIRLWIND

Jack Nicholson, Millie Perkins, Cameron Mitchell, Rupert Crosse. In **Ride in the Whirlwind**
Written by Jack Nicholson, Directed by Monte Hellman. Produced by Monte Hellman & Jack Nicholson

ON THE SET OF 'THE SHOOTING' (1965)
Two black hats: Jack as an enigmatic stranger with an equally mysterious woman (Millie Perkins). Filmed near Zion National Park, Utah. / Zweimal schwarzer Hut: Nicholson als rätselhafter Fremder mit einer nicht weniger rätselhaften Frau (Millie Perkins). Der Film wurde in der Nähe des Zion-Nationalparks in Utah gedreht. / Deux chapeaux noirs : Nicholson joue un étranger énigmatique aux côtés d'une femme non moins mystérieuse (Millie Perkins). Tourné près du Parc national de Zion (Utah).

POSTER FOR 'RIDE IN THE WHIRLWIND' (1965)
Jack is a cowboy mistaken for an outlaw and threatened with hanging in this existentialist western. / In diesem existenzialistischen Western spielt Nicholson einen Cowboy, den man irrtümlich für einen Gesetzlosen hält und deshalb aufknüpfen will. / Dans ce western existentialiste, Nicholson est un cow-boy pris pour un hors-la-loi et menacé de pendaison.

**STILL FROM
'HELLS ANGELS ON WHEELS' (1967)**
Jack plays a rebel biker who smiles through the pain as
he is beaten up by sailors. / Nicholson spielt einen
aufsässigen Motorradfahrer, dem auch dann nicht das
Grinsen vergeht, als er von Matrosen brutal
zusammengeschlagen wird. / Nicholson incarne un
motard rebelle qui garde le sourire alors qu'il se fait
tabasser par des marins.

**STILL FROM
'THE ST. VALENTINE'S DAY MASSACRE' (1967)**
Jack (right) in a bit part as a mob gangster in 1920s
Chicago. / Nicholson (rechts) spielt eine kleine
Nebenrolle als Mafiakiller im Chicago der 1920er-
Jahre. / Nicholson (à droite) dans un petit rôle de
gangster dans le Chicago des années 1920.

*"It's garlic. The bullet don't kill you. You die of
blood poisoning."*
Gino, the Hit Man (Jack Nicholson) on the practice of
greasing bullets, *The St. Valentine's Day Massacre* (1967)

*„Es ist Knoblauch. Die Kugel bringt dich nicht um.
Du stirbst an Blutvergiftung."*
Der Profikiller Gino (Jack Nicholson) über seine
Gewohnheit, Patronen mit Knoblauch einzureiben,
Chicago-Massaker (1967)

*« C'est de l'ail. Ce n'est pas la balle qui te tue.
Tu meurs d'un empoisonnement du sang. »*
Gino, le tueur à gages (Jack Nicholson), à propos de
sa technique de lubrification des balles, *L'Affaire
Al Capone* (1967)

> "The whole thing is to keep working, and pretty soon they'll think you're good."
> Jack Nicholson

> „Wichtig ist, dass du ständig arbeitest. Dann wird man bald von dir denken, du seist gut."
> Jack Nicholson

> « Le tout est de continuer à travailler, et très vite, ils finissent par te trouver bon. »
> Jack Nicholson

STILL FROM 'HEAD' (1968)

A rollicking satire on the marketing of The Monkees as a pop phenomenon. Jack cowrote the script. / Eine übermütige Satire über die Vermarktung der Band „The Monkees" als Popphänomen. Nicholson war Mitautor des Drehbuchs. / Une satire exubérante sur la manière dont le groupe The Monkees devint un phénomène de la culture pop. Nicholson coécrit le scénario.

STILL FROM 'PSYCH-OUT' (1968)
Jack as Stoney, hippie member of a psychedelic band,
with a friend (Adam Roarke). / Nicholson als Hippie
Stoney, Mitglied einer psychedelischen Band, mit einem
Freund (Adam Roarke). / Nicholson dans le rôle de
Stoney, membre hippie d'un groupe psychédélique,
avec un ami (Adam Roarke).

PAGES 40/41
STILL FROM 'EASY RIDER' (1969)
With Dennis Hopper alongside, Jack rides behind Peter
Fonda on a motorcycle trip across America. (He broke
one of Fonda's ribs holding on to him.) / Mit Dennis
Hopper an seiner Seite fährt Nicholson hinter Peter
Fonda auf dem Motorrad quer durch Amerika (und
brach dabei eine von Fondas Rippen). / Derrière Dennis
Hopper, Nicholson suit Peter Fonda dans un voyage en
moto à travers les États-Unis. (Il cassera une côte à
Fonda pendant le tournage.)

STILL FROM 'EASY RIDER' (1969)
As disillusioned ACLU lawyer George Hanson
in the film that made Jack a star. / Als desillusionierter
Rechtsanwalt der Bürgerrechtsorganisation ACLU in
jenem Film, der Nicholson zum Star machte. / George
Hanson est un avocat désenchanté de l'ACLU (« Union
américaine pour les libertés civiques ») dans le film qui
hisse Nicholson au rang de star.

*"This used to be a damn good country. I can't
figure out what happened to it."*
George Hanson (Jack Nicholson), *Easy Rider* (1969)

*„Das hier war mal ein verdammt gutes Land.
Ich kann mir einfach nicht erklären, was damit
passiert ist."*
George Hanson (Jack Nicholson), *Easy Rider* (1969)

*« Ce pays était rudement bien autrefois. Je n'arrive
pas à comprendre ce qui lui est arrivé. »*
George Hanson (Jack Nicholson), *Easy Rider* (1969)

**STILL FROM 'ON A CLEAR DAY
YOU CAN SEE FOREVER' (1970)**
Jack plays a hippie, but he still had to get a haircut for
his role in this Barbra Streisand musical. (His song solo
was removed from the final cut.) / Nicholson spielt zwar
einen Hippie, aber für seine Rolle in diesem Barbra-
Streisand-Musical musste er sich dennoch die Haare
stutzen lassen. (Und sein Gesangssolo fiel auch noch
der Schere zum Opfer!) / Nicholson joue un hippie, mais
il doit quand même passer entre les mains d'un coiffeur
pour ce rôle musical avec Barbra Streisand. (Sa chanson
en solo sera coupée au montage.)

"I move around a lot, not because I'm looking for anything really, but 'cause I'm getting away from things that get bad if I stay."
Bobby Dupea (Jack Nicholson), *Five Easy Pieces* **(1970)**

„Ich ziehe viel umher. Nicht weil ich wirklich auf der Suche nach irgendwas bin, sondern weil ich vor Dingen davonlaufe, die schlecht werden, wenn ich bleibe."
Bobby Dupea (Jack Nicholson), *Ein Mann sucht sich selbst* **(1970)**

« Je bouge beaucoup, pas vraiment parce que je cherche quelque chose, mais parce que je fuis les choses qui seraient pires encore si je restais. »
Bobby Dupea (Jack Nicholson), *Cinq pièces faciles* **(1970)**

STILL FROM 'FIVE EASY PIECES' (1970)
Oil-rigger or concert pianist? Country music or classical? Bobby Dupea (Nicholson) is torn between worlds. / Soll er nach Öl bohren oder Klavierkonzerte geben? Countrymusic oder Klassik? Bobby Dupea (Nicholson) ist zwischen zwei Welten hin- und hergerissen. / Ouvrier sur une plate-forme pétrolière ou pianiste ? Musique country ou classique ? Bobby Dupea (Nicholson) est déchiré entre deux mondes.

ON THE SET OF 'FIVE EASY PIECES' (1970)
With director Bob Rafelson. Jack said he would act for
Rafelson again anytime, and they eventually made five
films together. / Mit Regisseur Bob Rafelson. Nicholson
sagte schon damals, er würde jederzeit wieder mit
Rafelson zusammenarbeiten, und am Ende drehten
die beiden gemeinsam fünf Filme. / Avec le réalisateur
Bob Rafelson. Nicholson déclare qu'il aura plaisir à
retravailler avec Rafelson quand il le souhaitera.
Ils tourneront cinq films ensemble.

STILL FROM 'FIVE EASY PIECES' (1970)
Diner waitress Rayette (Karen Black) tries to get free-spirited Bobby to settle down with her. / Die Bedienung Rayette (Karen Black) versucht, den Freigeist Bobby zu überreden, bei ihr sesshaft zu werden. / La serveuse Rayette (Karen Black) essaie de convaincre le libre penseur Bobby de s'installer avec elle.

PAGES 48/49
STILL FROM 'FIVE EASY PIECES' (1970)
Bobby has an affair with his brother's fiancée, Catherine (Susan Anspach). Jack's real-life relationship with Anspach resulted in a son. / Bobby hat eine Affäre mit Catherine (Susan Anspach), der Verlobten seines Bruders. Aus Nicholsons Beziehung mit Anspach ging im wahren Leben ein Sohn hervor. / Bobby a une aventure avec la fiancée de son frère, Catherine (Susan Anspach). De la relation réelle entre Nicholson et Susan Anspach naîtra un fils.

*"I don't want people to know what I'm actually like.
It's not good for an actor."*
Jack Nicholson

*„Ich möchte nicht, dass die Leute wissen,
wie ich wirklich bin. Das ist nicht gut für einen
Schauspieler."*
Jack Nicholson

*« Je ne veux pas que les gens sachent qui je suis
vraiment. Ce n'est pas bon pour un acteur. »*
Jack Nicholson

ON THE SET OF 'DRIVE, HE SAID' (1971)
Jack's directorial debut. The film's full-frontal nudity
and bold depiction of the sex act saddled it with an
X rating. / Nicholsons Debüt auf dem Regiestuhl.
Die Nacktszenen des Films und die gewagte Darstellung
des Geschlechtsverkehrs brachten dem Film ein
Jugendverbot ein. / Les débuts de Nicholson comme
réalisateur. La nudité totale et les scènes d'amour très
crues valent au film d'être classé X.

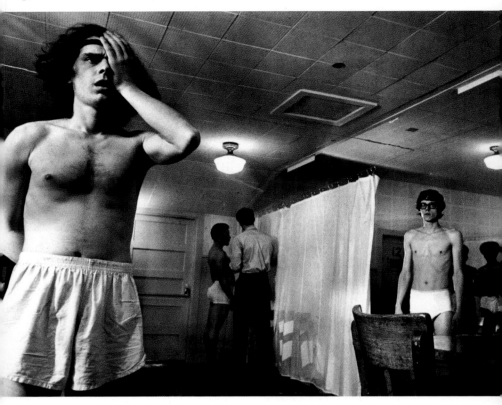

STILL FROM 'DRIVE, HE SAID' (1971)
To avoid Vietnam, campus radical Gabriel (Michael
Margotta) will feign insanity at his draft board. / Um sich
vor Vietnam zu drücken, täuscht der Radikale Gabriel
(Michael Margotta) bei der Musterung vor,
geistesgestört zu sein. / Pour éviter le Vietnam,
l'étudiant engagé Gabriel (Michael Margotta) feint
la folie devant le conseil de révision militaire...

"My thought is that I should try and do what other
people can't do. I should be very esoteric and hope
it will communicate."
Jack Nicholson on choosing his film roles

„Ich denke mir, ich sollte versuchen, das zu tun, was
andere nicht können. Ich sollte sehr esoterisch sein
und hoffen, es kommt rüber."
Jack Nicholson über die Auswahl seiner Filmrollen

« Mon idée, c'est que je devrais essayer de faire ce
que les autres ne savent pas faire. Agir de façon
très ésotérique et espérer réussir à communiquer
ce que je veux. »
Jack Nicholson à propos du choix de ses rôles

STILL FROM 'DRIVE, HE SAID' (1971)
But the drugs Gabriel has taken drive him insane. /
Doch die Drogen, die Gabriel genommen hat, treiben
ihn tatsächlich in den Wahnsinn. / Mais les drogues que
Gabriel a prises le rendent réellement fou.

PAGES 54/55
ON THE SET OF 'DRIVE, HE SAID' (1971)
Coaching young actor William Tepper on how to play a
college basketball star. (Jack is a longtime L.A. Lakers
basketball fan.) / Regisseur Nicholson zeigt dem
Jungschauspieler William Tepper, wie man einen
College-Basketball-Star spielt. (Nicholson ist seit
Langem ein Fan der L.A. Lakers.) / Nicholson donne des
conseils au jeune acteur William Tepper sur la manière
de jouer une vedette de basket universitaire (il suit
depuis longtemps avec passion les saisons des Lakers
de Los Angeles).

STILL FROM 'DRIVE, HE SAID' (1971)
Jack directs Karen Black in order to get just the right reaction shot. / Nicholson gibt Karen Black Regieanweisungen, um genau den richtigen Gegenschuss zu erhalten. / Nicholson dirige Karen Black pour obtenir précisément la réaction qu'il recherche.

"He is more hip than any man I know. I've never known anyone who enjoyed being himself more than Jack. He brings out the child in himself and everyone else."
Mark Canton, film executive

„Er ist hipper als irgendein anderer Mensch, den ich kenne. Ich habe nie jemanden kennengelernt, der mehr Spaß daran hatte, er selbst zu sein, als Jack. Er bringt das Kind, das in ihm und jedem anderen Menschen steckt, zum Vorschein."
Mark Canton, Produzent und Vorstand einer Filmfirma

ON THE SET OF 'DRIVE, HE SAID' (1971)
Karen Black meditates on her role as a professor's wife having an affair with a student. / Karen Black denkt über ihre Rolle als Professorengattin nach, die sich mit einem Studenten einlässt. / Karen Black médite sur son rôle, celui d'une femme de professeur qui a une aventure avec un de ses étudiants.

« Il est plus branché que tous les hommes que je connais. Je n'ai jamais rencontré personne qui soit aussi heureux d'être lui-même que Jack. Il sait faire ressortir l'enfant en lui, et en chacun de nous. »
Mark Canton, producteur exécutif

"Women today are better-hung than the men!"
Jonathan Fuerst (Jack Nicholson),
Carnal Knowledge (1971)

„*Die Frauen von heute haben mehr zwischen den
Beinen als die Männer!*"
Jonathan Fuerst (Jack Nicholson),
Die Kunst zu lieben (1971)

« *Aujourd'hui, les femmes sont mieux montées que
les hommes !* »
Jonathan Fuerst (Jack Nicholson),
Ce plaisir qu'on dit charnel (1971)

STILL FROM 'CARNAL KNOWLEDGE' (1971)
Sandy (Art Garfunkel) confronts Jonathan (Nicholson)
on how his compulsive womanizing only makes him
unhappy. / Sandy (Art Garfunkel) führt Jonathan
(Nicholson) vor Augen, wie dieser sich als zwanghafter
Schürzenjäger nur unglücklich macht. / Sandy
(Art Garfunkel) affronte Jonathan (Nicholson) pour lui
faire comprendre que sa consommation compulsive de
femmes ne fait que le rendre malheureux.

STILL FROM 'CARNAL KNOWLEDGE' (1971)
Bobbie (Ann-Margret) wants marriage, but Jonathan has his eyes on sexual conquest. / Bobbie (Ann-Margret) möchte heiraten, aber Jonathan geht es nur um die sexuelle Eroberung. / Bobbie (Ann-Margret) veut se marier, mais Jonathan est trop obsédé par les conquêtes sexuelles.

PAGES 60/61
STILL FROM 'A SAFE PLACE' (1971)
Jack improvised most of his role as a bohemian, with costar Tuesday Weld as a flower child. / Nicholson improvisierte den größten Teil seiner Rolle als Bohemien – hier mit Kollegin Tuesday Weld in der Rolle eines Blumenkinds. / Nicholson improvise en grande partie son rôle de bohémien ; ici avec Tuesday Weld en hippie.

**STILL FROM
'THE KING OF MARVIN GARDENS' (1972)**
David (Nicholson) interviews a beauty queen (Julia
Anne Robinson) for a mock Miss America pageant. /
David (Nicholson) interviewt eine Schönheitskönigin
(Julia Anne Robinson) für eine getürkte Miss-Wahl. /
David (Nicholson) interviewe une reine de beauté
(Julia Anne Robinson) pour un faux concours de
Miss Amérique.

*"I think the most impressive thing about me is that
I've done 20 to 25 films, and none of the characters
are alike."*
Jack Nicholson (1975)

*„Ich denke, das Eindrucksvollste an mir ist, dass ich
20 bis 25 Filme gemacht habe und keine der
Figuren wie die andere ist."*
Jack Nicholson (1975)

*« Ce qu'il y a de plus impressionnant à mon propos,
je pense, c'est que j'ai tourné 20 à 25 films et
qu'aucun de mes personnages ne ressemble à
un autre. »*
Jack Nicholson (1975)

**STILL FROM
'THE KING OF MARVIN GARDENS' (1972)**
Jack and Bruce Dern play brothers with opposite
temperaments. Off-screen they were longtime friends
and rivals for acting roles. / Jack Nicholson und Bruce
Dern spielen zwei Brüder mit gegensätzlichem
Temperament. Im Leben waren sie seit Jahren
befreundet und häufig Konkurrenten, wenn es um
bestimmte Rollen ging. / Jack Nicholson et Bruce
Dern jouent des frères aux caractères opposés.
Hors écran, ils sont amis et rivaux de longue date.

ON THE SET OF 'THE LAST DETAIL' (1973)
With director Hal Ashby (left) and costar Otis Young.
Script approval was delayed for two years due to the
profusion of obscene language. / Mit Regisseur Hal
Ashby (links) und Schauspielkollege Otis Young.
Aufgrund der Flut an Kraftausdrücken dauerte es zwei
Jahre, bis das Drehbuch genehmigt wurde. / Avec le
réalisateur Hal Ashby (à gauche) et son partenaire
Otis Young. En raison d'une profusion de mots
obscènes, il faudra deux ans avant que le scénario
passe la censure.

PORTRAIT FOR 'THE LAST DETAIL' (1973)
With cigar and tattooed bicep, Jack strikes a macho
pose as Billy "Bad Ass" Buddusky. / Mit Zigarre und
tätowiertem Bizeps spielt Nicholson als Billy „Bad Ass"
Buddusky einen Macho. / Cigare aux lèvres et biceps
tatoué, Nicholson se pose en macho dans le rôle de Billy
« Bad Ass » Buddusky.

*"I am the motherfucking shore patrol!
Give this man a beer!"*
Billy "Bad Ass" Buddusky (Jack Nicholson), *The Last
Detail* **(1973)**

*„Ich bin die beschissene Küstenpatrouille! Geben
Sie diesem Mann ein Bier!"*
Billy „Bad Ass" Buddusky (Jack Nicholson), *Das letzte
Kommando* **(1973)**

*« Je fais partie de cette putain de patrouille !
Donne une bière à ce type ! »*
Billy « Bad Ass » Buddusky (Jack Nicholson), *La Dernière
Corvée* **(1973)**

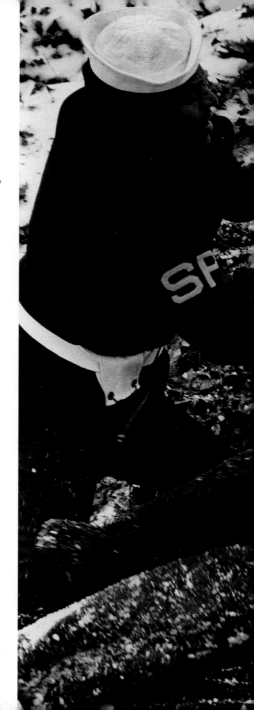

STILL FROM 'THE LAST DETAIL' (1973)
MPs Mulhall (Otis Young) and Buddusky must
eventually do their duty and haul Meadows (Randy
Quaid) to prison. / Die Feldjäger Mulhall (Otis Young)
und Buddusky müssen schließlich ihre Pflicht erfüllen
und Meadows (Randy Quaid) hinter Gitter bringen. /
Les agents Mulhall (Otis Young) et Buddusky sont
contraints de faire leur devoir et d'emmener Meadows
(Randy Quaid) en prison.

STILL FROM 'THE LAST DETAIL' (1973)
Rite of passage: Mulhall and Buddusky plan to show
Meadows a good time and make him a man before the
young sailor must spend eight years behind bars for
petty theft. / Initiationsritus: Mulhall und Buddusky
wollen, dass Meadows noch einmal Spaß hat und zum
Mann wird, bevor der junge Matrose wegen eines
kleinen Diebstahls für acht Jahre ins Gefängnis gehen
muss. / Rite de passage : Mulhall et Buddusky veulent
faire passer un bon moment à Meadows et faire de lui
un homme, avant que le jeune marin soit enfermé
pendant huit ans pour un menu larcin.

"You know, Jack, what the public likes about your characters is that you're always playing the guy who has this tremendous ability at any given moment to say, 'Why don't you go fuck yourself?'"
Billy Wilder, director

„Weißt du, Jack, was das Publikum an deinen Figuren mag, ist, dass du immer den Typen spielst, der diese ungeheure Fähigkeit besitzt, jederzeit zu sagen: ‚Warum leckst du mich nicht einfach am Arsch?'"
Billy Wilder, Regisseur

« Vous savez, Jack, ce que le public aime dans vos personnages, c'est que vous jouez toujours le gars qui a cette capacité incroyable de dire, à n'importe quel moment : "Pourquoi est-ce que vous n'allez pas vous faire foutre ?" »
Billy Wilder, réalisateur

STILL FROM 'THE LAST DETAIL' (1973)
This uncompromising film was a critical and commercial hit. / Dieser kompromisslose Film – *Das letzte Kommando* – war sowohl beim Publikum als auch bei den Kritikern ein Erfolg. / Ce film intransigeant – *La Dernière Corvée* – remporte un double succès critique et commercial.

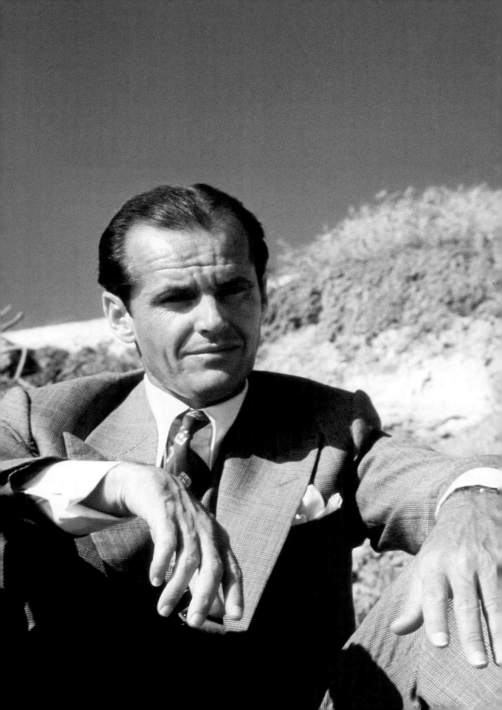

STILL FROM 'CHINATOWN' (1974)
A gangster slits Gittes's nose for being a "very nosy fellow." The gangster is director Roman Polanski in a cameo role. / Ein Gangster schlitzt Gittes die Nase auf, weil er zu „naseweis" ist. Den Kriminellen spielt Regisseur Roman Polanski in einer Cameo-Rolle. / Un gangster (interprété par le réalisateur Roman Polanski) coupe le nez de Gittes parce qu'il trouve qu'il le met un peu trop partout.

PORTRAIT FOR 'CHINATOWN' (1974)
Jack as dapper detective Jake Gittes—a modern-day Humphrey Bogart in this neo noir. / Nicholson als adretter Privatdetektiv Jake Gittes – ein moderner Humphrey Bogart in einem Neo-Film-noir. / Nicholson joue le très soigné détective Jake Gittes, un Humphrey Bogart moderne, dans ce film noir contemporain.

ON THE SET OF 'CHINATOWN' (1974)

Location shooting in dry California. The film actually manages to make something exciting out of a true-life dispute over water rights. / Außenaufnahmen im trockenen Kalifornien. Dem Film gelingt es tatsächlich, einem wahren Streit über Wasserrechte Spannung abzugewinnen. / Tournage en décors naturels dans la sèche Californie. Le film parvient à rendre passionnante une dispute concernant des droits d'accès à l'eau.

PORTRAIT FOR 'CHINATOWN' (1974)

The least vain of actors, Jack played much of this part with an ugly bandage taped over his nose. / Nicholson, der Uneitelste unter den Schauspielern, spielte den größten Teil seiner Rolle mit einem hässlichen Pflaster auf der Nase. / Acteur tout sauf vaniteux, Nicholson passe la majeure partie du film avec un horrible pansement au milieu du visage.

STILL FROM 'CHINATOWN' (1974)
The wrong man: Jake is beaten up by farmers who mistakenly blame him for their troubles. / Der falsche Mann: Jake wird von Bauern verprügelt, die ihm fälschlicherweise die Schuld an ihrer Misere geben. / Le bouc émissaire : Jake est passé à tabac par des fermiers qui le jugent responsable de leurs problèmes.

PAGES 76/77
STILL FROM 'CHINATOWN' (1974)
With costar Faye Dunaway. This is the film in which Jack graduated from character roles to leading man. / Mit Kollegin Faye Dunaway. Mit diesem Film schaffte Nicholson den Sprung von den Charakterrollen zum Hauptdarsteller. / Avec sa partenaire Faye Dunaway. Grâce à ce film, Nicholson passe des personnages marquants au personnage principal.

STILL FROM 'CHINATOWN' (1974)
Gittes slaps Evelyn Mulwray (Faye Dunaway) to get the truth. After several fake slaps didn't look real enough, Dunaway had Jack actually strike her. / Gittes ohrfeigt Evelyn Mulwray (Faye Dunaway), um die Wahrheit zu erfahren. Nach mehreren vorgetäuschten Backpfeifen, die nicht echt genug aussahen, ließ sich Dunaway von Nicholson tatsächlich schlagen. / Gittes gifle Evelyn Mulwray (Faye Dunaway) pour obtenir la vérité. Après plusieurs fausses claques qui n'avaient pas l'air suffisamment vraies, Dunaway demande à Nicholson de porter son coup.

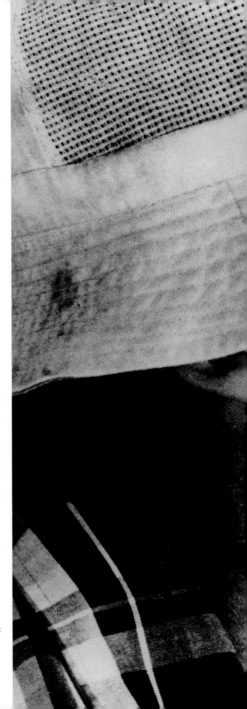

"If you get an impulse in a scene, no matter how wrong it seems, follow the impulse. It might be something, and if it ain't—take two!"
Jack Nicholson

„Wenn du bei einer Szene eine Eingebung verspürst, ganz gleich, wie unpassend sie erscheinen mag, dann folge ihr. Vielleicht ist ja was dran, und wenn nicht – dann gibt's eben Take two!"
Jack Nicholson

« Si vous avez une impulsion pendant une scène, aussi mauvaise qu'elle paraisse, suivez cette impulsion. Elle pourrait vous mener quelque part, et si ce n'est pas le cas – faites une pause ! »
Jack Nicholson

STILL FROM 'THE PASSENGER' (1975)
Jack made this film because he wanted to work with legendary art-house director Michelangelo Antonioni. / Nicholson drehte diesen Film, weil er unbedingt mit Regielegende Michelangelo Antonioni arbeiten wollte. / Nicholson fait ce film parce qu'il veut travailler avec Michelangelo Antonioni, la légende italienne du cinéma expérimental.

PAGES 80/81
STILL FROM 'THE PASSENGER' (1975)
The Sahara Desert setting prompts David Locke (Nicholson) to look inward and examine the question of man's identity. / Die Wüstenkulisse der Sahara veranlasst David Locke (Nicholson), in sich hineinzuhorchen und Fragen der menschlichen Identität zu erforschen. / Le désert du Sahara qui l'entoure pousse David Locke (Nicholson) à l'introspection; il s'interroge sur ce qui fait l'identité d'un homme.

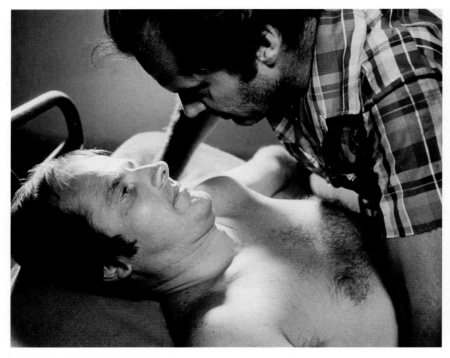

STILL FROM 'THE PASSENGER' (1975)
David switches identities with a dead look-alike and
begins to live the other man's life. / David schlüpft in die
Rolle eines toten Doppelgängers und beginnt, das
Leben des Anderen zu leben. / David prend l'identité
d'un mort qui lui ressemble et se met à vivre la vie de
cet homme.

STILL FROM 'THE PASSENGER' (1975)
The Girl (Maria Schneider): "People disappear every
day." David: "Every time they leave the room." / Das
Mädchen (Maria Schneider): „Menschen verschwinden
jeden Tag." David: „Jedes Mal, wenn sie das Zimmer
verlassen." / La fille (Maria Schneider) : « Des gens
disparaissent tous les jours. » David : « À chaque fois
qu'ils quittent une pièce. »

"I used to be someone else,
but I traded him in."
David Locke (Jack Nicholson), *The Passenger* **(1975)**

„Ich war mal jemand anderer,
aber ich hab ihn eingetauscht."
David Locke (Jack Nicholson), *Beruf: Reporter* **(1975)**

« Avant, j'étais quelqu'un d'autre,
mais je l'ai échangé. »
David Locke (Jack Nicholson), *Profession : reporter* **(1975)**

STILL FROM 'THE PASSENGER' (1975)
Does David take on another man's identity as a flight
from his own personal problems? / Nimmt David die
Identität eines Fremden an, um vor seinen eigenen
persönlichen Problemen zu fliehen? / David endosse-t-il
l'identité d'un autre homme pour fuir ses propres
problèmes ?

STILL FROM 'THE PASSENGER' (1975)
Mystery woman: Is the girl a life-loving hippie or a
femme fatale? / Die Geheimnisvolle: Ist das Mädchen
ein lebensfroher Hippie oder eine Femme fatale? /
La femme mystère : la fille est-elle une hippie assoiffée
d'amour ou une femme fatale ?

PORTRAIT FOR 'THE FORTUNE' (1975)

After the seriously adult ménage à trois of *Carnal Knowledge* Jack found a darker threesome with Stockard Channing and Warren Beatty in this screwball comedy. / Nach der ernsthaften Dreierbeziehung unter Erwachsenen in *Die Kunst zu lieben* fand Nicholson einen düstereren Dreier mit Stockard Channing und Warren Beatty in dieser Screwball-Komödie. / Après le ménage à trois sans fard de Ce *plaisir qu'on dit charnel*, Nicholson se frotte à une partie à trois plus sombre encore dans cette comédie déjantée, avec Stockard Channing et Warren Beatty.

PORTRAIT FOR 'THE FORTUNE' (1975)

STILL FROM 'ONE FLEW OVER THE CUCKOO'S NEST' (1975)
To avoid prison-work detail, McMurphy (Nicholson) acts crazy so that he is sent to a mental hospital. / Um keine Zwangsarbeit leisten zu müssen, spielt McMurphy (Nicholson) verrückt, damit man ihn in eine Nervenheilanstalt einweist. / Pour éviter la prison et les travaux forcés, McMurphy (Nicholson) simule la folie dans l'espoir d'être interné.

STILL FROM 'ONE FLEW OVER THE CUCKOO'S NEST' (1975)
For his tour de force performance, Jack won his first Oscar for best actor—after being nominated three times before. / Für diese schauspielerische Meisterleistung erhielt Nicholson nach drei vorausgegangenen Nominierungen endlich seinen ersten Oscar als bester Hauptdarsteller. / Grâce à une interprétation qui a tout du tour de force, Nicholson remporte son premier oscar du Meilleur acteur ; il a déjà été nominé trois fois.

**STILL FROM 'ONE FLEW
OVER THE CUCKOO'S NEST' (1975)**
McMurphy defies the rule-bound Nurse Ratched
(Louise Fletcher), who walls herself off behind glass. /
McMurphy bietet der streng nach Vorschrift
arbeitenden Krankenschwester Ratched (Louise
Fletcher), die sich hinter einer Glasscheibe verschanzt,
die Stirn. / McMurphy défie la rêche infirmière Ratched
(Louise Fletcher), qui se protège derrière une
éternelle vitre.

**POSTER FOR 'ONE FLEW
OVER THE CUCKOO'S NEST' (1975)**
This Turkish poster for the film makes McMurphy look
like a madman in a horror movie. / Auf diesem
türkischen Filmplakat wirkt McMurphy eher wie ein
Psychopath in einem Horrorfilm. / Sur cette affiche
turque pour le film, McMurphy ressemble à un dément
de film d'horreur.

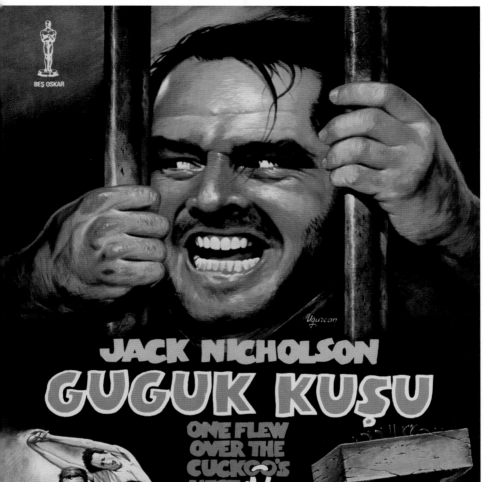

BEŞ OSKAR

JACK NICHOLSON

GUGUK KUŞU

ONE FLEW
OVER THE
CUCKOO'S
NEST

Yönetmen:
MILOS FORMAN

United Artists

ÖZENFİLM

RENKLİ - TÜRKÇE

"Which one of you nuts has got any guts?"
Randle Patrick McMurphy (Jack Nicholson), *One Flew
Over the Cuckoo's Nest* (1975)

„Wer von euch Bekloppten hat Mumm?"
Randle Patrick McMurphy (Jack Nicholson), *Einer flog
über das Kuckucksnest* (1975)

« Allez les fous, soyez pas mous ! »
Randle Patrick McMurphy (Jack Nicholson), *Vol au-dessus
d'un nid de coucou* (1975)

**STILL FROM 'ONE FLEW
OVER THE CUCKOO'S NEST' (1975)**
McMurphy inspires the mental patients to rebel against
their drugged hospital routine. / McMurphy stiftet die
Patienten der Anstalt zum Aufstand gegen die ständige
Ruhigstellung durch Medikamente an. / McMurphy
encourage les patients à se révolter contre la routine
hospitalière et le piège des médicaments.

STILL FROM 'THE MISSOURI BREAKS' (1976)
Jack jumped at the chance to work with his longtime
idol (and next-door neighbor), Marlon Brando. /
Nicholson packte die Gelegenheit beim Schopf, mit
dem von ihm seit Langem verehrten Idol Marlon Brando
zu arbeiten, der zudem sein Nachbar war. / Nicholson
saute sur l'occasion de travailler avec son idole de
toujours (et son voisin d'à-côté), Marlon Brando.

PAGES 96/97
STILL FROM 'GOIN' SOUTH' (1978)
Henry Moon (Nicholson) holds the stagecoach at
gunpoint, but his bride (Mary Steenburgen) has her rifle
trained on him! / Henry Moon (Nicholson) hält die
Kutscher in Schach, aber seine Braut (Mary
Steenburgen) hat ihr Gewehr auf ihn gerichtet! / Henry
Moon (Nicholson) tient la diligence en joue, mais son
épouse (Mary Steenburgen) pointe son arme sur lui!

STILL FROM 'THE MISSOURI BREAKS' (1976)
Jack enjoys a rare moment of musical peace in this
offbeat western scripted by cult novelist Thomas
McGuane. / Nicholson genießt eine seltene
Verschnaufpause an seiner Klarinette in diesem
schrägen Western nach einem Drehbuch des
Kultschriftstellers Thomas McGuane. / Nicholson
savoure un rare moment de paix en musique dans ce
western débridé écrit par le célèbre romancier Thomas
McGuane.

STILL FROM 'GOIN' SOUTH' (1978)
Horse thief Henry wants to be saved from the hangman, but is there a fate worse than death? / Der Pferdedieb Henry (Nicholson) würde gerne den Kopf aus der Schlinge ziehen – aber gibt es vielleicht noch ein Schicksal, das schlimmer ist als der Strick? / Henry, le voleur de chevaux, veut échapper à la potence, mais n'y a-t-il pas pire sort que la mort ?

PORTRAIT FOR 'GOIN' SOUTH' (1978)
Impish Jack is both director and star of this romantic comedy set in the Wild West. / Der verschmitzte Nicholson spielte nicht nur die Hauptrolle, sondern führte auch Regie in dieser Wildwest-Liebeskomödie. / L'espiègle Nicholson est le réalisateur et l'acteur vedette de cette comédie romantique à la sauce western.

STILL FROM 'GOIN' SOUTH' (1978)
The only way that Henry can escape the gallows is to
get married. Here the lady (Mary Steenburgen) and the
outlaw tie the knot. / Nur durch eine Heirat kann Henry
dem Galgen entkommen. In dieser Szene geben sich die
Dame (Mary Steenburgen) und der Bandit das Jawort. /
La seule manière pour Henry d'échapper à la mort est
de se marier. Ici, la dame (Mary Steenburgen) et le
brigand franchissent le pas.

*"He makes mischief and evil the most charming
things in the world."*
Actress Susan Anspach on Jack Nicholson

*„Bei ihm werden Unfug und Unheil zu den
entzückendsten Dingen der Welt."*
Schauspielerin Susan Anspach über Jack Nicholson

*« Il fait de la malice et du mal les choses les plus
charmantes du monde. »*
L'actrice Susan Anspach à propos de Jack Nicholson

STILL FROM 'GOIN' SOUTH' (1978)
"How's about a little dessert?" The randy Henry has a
craving for his new bride. / „Wie wär's mit 'nem kleinen
Nachtisch?" Dem geilen Henry gelüstet nach seiner
Frischangetrauten. / « Et si on passait au dessert ? »
Henry, d'humeur lubrique, consommerait bien la
jeune mariée.

ON THE SET OF 'THE SHINING' (1980)

A wife tries to fend off her homicidal husband. Nicholson was eager to act for renowned director Stanley Kubrick. / Eine Frau versucht, sich gegen ihren mordlüsternen Ehemann zu wehren. Nicholson wollte unbedingt für den angesehenen Regisseur Stanley Kubrick arbeiten. / Une épouse tentant de repousser son assassin de mari. Nicholson avait hâte de travailler pour le célèbre réalisateur Stanley Kubrick.

STILL FROM 'THE SHINING' (1980)
Jack Torrance (Nicholson) already looks a little crazed as he drives his family (Shelley Duvall, Danny Lloyd) up to the Colorado mountains. / Schon als er mit seiner Familie (Shelley Duvall, Danny Lloyd) in die Berge von Colorado fährt, scheint Jack Torrance (Nicholson) etwas auszubrüten. / Jack Torrance (Nicholson) a déjà l'air un peu atteint alors qu'il conduit sa famille (Shelley Duvall, Danny Lloyd) jusqu'aux sommets du Colorado.

PAGES 104/105
STILL FROM 'THE SHINING' (1980)
Haunted hotel: Is Lloyd the bartender really there or is Torrance looking at a reflection of his own desire for a drink? / Das Spukhotel in den Bergen: Ist Barmann Lloyd tatsächlich anwesend, oder sieht Torrance nur die Spiegelung seines eigenen Verlangens nach einem Drink? / L'hôtel hanté : Lloyd le barman est-il vraiment là, ou Torrance voit-il un reflet de son propre désir d'alcool ?

PAGES 106/107
STILL FROM 'THE SHINING' (1980)
With head down and eyes up, Jack gives his iconic evil look. This is the first of his over-the-top villain roles. / Mit gesenktem Kopf und nach oben gerichteten Augen zeigt Nicholson seinen typischen „bösen Blick". Hier spielt er zum ersten Mal einen völlig überzogenen Bösewicht. / Front baissé et regard par-dessous, Nicholson et son visage le plus maléfique. Ce rôle inaugure une série de méchants hors du commun.

**STILL FROM 'THE POSTMAN
ALWAYS RINGS TWICE' (1981)**
As a Depression-era drifter who encounters some cruel
turns of fate. / In der Zeit der Weltwirtschaftskrise
erlebt Frank ein paar grausame Wendungen des
Schicksals. / Vagabond pendant la Grande Dépression,
Frank subit une série de cruels coups du sort.

**PORTRAIT FOR 'THE POSTMAN
ALWAYS RINGS TWICE' (1981)**
Frank (Nicholson) falls for a woman who entices him to
murder in this raunchy remake of a classic film noir. / In
diesem Remake eines Klassikers des Film noir verliebt
sich Frank (Nicholson) in eine Frau, die ihn dazu
verleitet, einen Mord zu begehen. / Frank (Nicholson)
tombe sous le charme d'une femme qui le pousse au
meurtre dans cette nouvelle version torride d'un film
noir classique.

PAGES 110/111
**STILL FROM 'THE POSTMAN
ALWAYS RINGS TWICE' (1981)**
The film's sex scenes between Jack and Jessica Lange
were so steamy that it was rumored they were doing it
for real. / Die Sexszenen des Films zwischen Jack
Nicholson und Jessica Lange waren so erotisch, dass
gemunkelt wurde, sie seien nicht gespielt. / Les scènes
d'amour entre Jack Nicholson et Jessica Lange sont si
chaudes qu'on les a dites réelles.

STILL FROM 'THE BORDER' (1982)
Border patrolman Charlie Smith (Nicholson) fights police corruption and feels the plight of illegal immigrants. / Der Grenzpolizist Charlie Smith (Nicholson) bekämpft die Korruption in den eigenen Reihen und empfindet Mitleid für die illegalen Einwanderer. / L'agent de la police des frontières Charlie Smith (Nicholson) combat la corruption policière et comprend la détresse des immigrants illégaux.

STILL FROM 'THE BORDER' (1982)
For this film, Jack returned to subtle, naturalistic acting. Director Tony Richardson told him, "Less is more." / In diesem Film kehrte Nicholson wieder zu einer zurückhaltenden, natürlichen Art des Schauspielens zurück. Regisseur Tony Richardson mahnte ihn: „Weniger ist mehr." / Pour ce film, Nicholson revient à un jeu subtil et naturaliste. Le réalisateur Tony Richardson lui donne une consigne de sobriété : « Moins, c'est mieux. »

STILL FROM 'TERMS OF ENDEARMENT' (1983)
Shirley MacLaine on Jack's willingness to show his
paunchy belly in the bedroom scene: "I adore the fact
you don't care how you look." / Shirley MacLaine über
Nicholsons Bereitschaft, in der Bettszene seine Wampe
in die Kamera zu halten: „Ich bewundere die Tatsache,
dass es dir gleichgültig ist, wie du aussiehst." / Shirley
MacLaine, à propos de la volonté de Nicholson de
montrer son ventre bedonnant dans une scène
d'amour : « J'adore le fait que tu te fiches de ce dont
tu as l'air. »

STILL FROM 'TERMS OF ENDEARMENT' (1983)
Ex-astronaut Garrett Breedlove (Nicholson) shows
uptight widow Aurora (Shirley MacLaine) how to let
loose and fly. / Der ehemalige Astronaut Garrett
Breedlove (Nicholson) zeigt der zugeknöpften Witwe
Aurora (Shirley MacLaine), wie es ist, wenn man sich
gehen lässt und abhebt. / L'ancien astronaute Garrett
Breedlove (Nicholson) montre à une veuve coincée,
Aurora (Shirley MacLaine), comment se laisser aller
et s'envoler.

STILL FROM 'PRIZZI'S HONOR' (1985)
Dark comedy: Charley wonders, "Do I ice her? Do I marry her? Which one of these?" / Schwarzer Humor: Charley fragt sich: „Soll ich sie umlegen? Soll ich sie heiraten? Wofür soll ich mich entscheiden?" / Dans cette comédie noire, Charley se demande : « Je la liquide ? Je l'épouse ? Qu'est-ce que je fais ? »

STILL FROM 'PRIZZI'S HONOR' (1985)
Hit man Charley Partanna (Nicholson) falls for a beautiful lady (Kathleen Turner) who turns out to be a hit woman! / Der Auftragskiller Charley Partanna (Nicholson) verliebt sich in die hübsche Dame (Kathleen Turner), die sich als Kollegin erweist! / Le tueur Charley Partanna (Nicholson) tombe amoureux d'une très belle femme (Kathleen Turner) qui se révèle être aussi une tueuse !

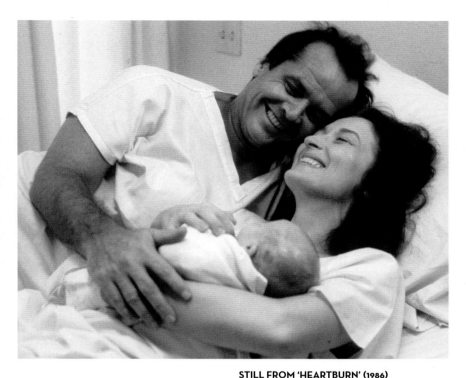

STILL FROM 'HEARTBURN' (1986)
Bittersweet marriage: Mark (Nicholson) is a fond
father—but a philandering husband. / Bittersüße Ehe:
Mark (Nicholson) ist ein liebender Vater – aber ein
untreuer Ehemann. / Mariage doux-amer : Mark
(Nicholson) est un père affectueux, mais un mari
coureur.

STILL FROM 'HEARTBURN' (1986)
Meryl Streep with Jack. Script by Nora Ephron based
on her real-life breakup with Watergate reporter Carl
Bernstein. / Meryl Streep mit Nicholson. Das Drehbuch
von Nora Ephron basierte auf ihrer eigenen Trennung
von Watergate-Reporter Carl Bernstein. / Meryl Streep
avec Nicholson. Le scénario de Nora Ephron s'inspire de
sa propre rupture avec le journaliste du Watergate
Carl Bernstein.

PAGES 120/121
**STILL FROM
'THE WITCHES OF EASTWICK' (1987)**
Mystery man Daryl Van Horne seems to satisfy
every appetite of three bored housewives. /
Der undurchsichtige Daryl Van Horne scheint jeden
Appetit der drei gelangweilten Hausfrauen zu stillen. /
Le mystérieux Daryl Van Horne semble satisfaire tous
les appétits de ces femmes au foyer en proie à l'ennui.

**STILL FROM
'THE WITCHES OF EASTWICK' (1987)**
"He's fat, old, losing his hair and he still pulls the chicks.
He's a hero for an ageing population that badly wants
to feel sexy."—Robert Leedham on Jack Nicholson /
„Er ist fett, alt, verliert seine Haare und schleppt
immer noch die Miezen ab. Er ist der Held einer
alternden Bevölkerung, die danach lechzt, sich sexy
zu fühlen." — Robert Leedham über Jack Nicholson /
« Il est gros, vieux, il perd ses cheveux, et il lève toujours
les poulettes. C'est un héros pour la population
vieillissante qui a si désespérément envie de se sentir
sexy. » — Robert Leedham à propos de Jack Nicholson

**PORTRAIT FOR
'THE WITCHES OF EASTWICK' (1987)**
Posing with the three "witches" who conjured him up:
Michelle Pfeiffer, Susan Sarandon, and Cher. / Daryl
posiert mit den drei „Hexen", die ihn riefen: Michelle
Pfeiffer, Susan Sarandon und Cher. / Pose avec les trois
« sorcières » qui ont su le conjurer : Michelle Pfeiffer,
Susan Sarandon et Cher.

**STILL FROM
'THE WITCHES OF EASTWICK' (1987)**
Daryl's male-chauvinistic outcry: "Women—a mistake, or
did He do it to us on purpose?" / Daryls männlich-
chauvinistischer Verzweiflungsschrei: „Frauen – ein
Fehler! Oder hat ‚Er' uns das absichtlich angetan?" /
Le cri du cœur de Daryl : « Les femmes ? Une erreur...
Ou peut-être qu'il l'a fait exprès ? »

PAGES 124/125
**STILL FROM
'THE WITCHES OF EASTWICK' (1987)**
When dream date Daryl is revealed to be a misogynistic
devil, the women cause a storm of feathers to blow him
into church. / Als sich Traumpartner Daryl als
frauenfeindlicher Teufel erweist, zaubern die Frauen
einen Federsturm herbei, der ihn in die Kirche blasen
soll. / Lorsque Daryl le gendre idéal se révèle un démon
misogyne, les femmes provoquent une tempête de
plumes qui l'expédie à l'intérieur de l'église.

"I'm just your average horny little devil!"
Daryl Van Horne (Jack Nicholson), *The Witches of
Eastwick* (1987)

*„Ich bin nur euer kleines geiles
Durchschnittsteufelchen!"*
Daryl Van Horne (Jack Nicholson), *Die Hexen von
Eastwick* (1987)

« Je ne suis qu'un petit démon lubrique moyen ! »
Daryl Van Horne (Jack Nicholson), *Les Sorcières
d'Eastwick* (1987)

ON THE SET OF
'THE WITCHES OF EASTWICK' (1987)
The grotesque model used for the climax where Daryl
rampages in his true form as an ugly devil. / Dieses
groteske Modell wurde für den Höhepunkt des Films
verwendet, als Daryl in seiner wahren Form als
hässlicher Teufel Amok läuft. / Le mannequin grotesque
utilisé pour la scène où Daryl dévoile sa forme
diabolique.

STILL FROM 'IRONWEED' (1987)

After *Heartburn*, Meryl Streep was eager to work
with Nicholson again: "I really admire him, because he
isn't afraid of anything." / Nach *Sodbrennen* wollte
Meryl Streep unbedingt erneut mit Nicholson arbeiten:
„Ich bewundere ihn wirklich, weil er sich vor nichts
fürchtet." / Après *La Brûlure*, Meryl Streep avait hâte
de travailler à nouveau avec Nicholson : « Je l'admire
vraiment, parce qu'il n'a peur de rien. »

STILL FROM 'IRONWEED' (1987)
Jack bravely took on this less-than-endearing part as an alcoholic haunted by the dark deeds in his past. / Nicholson schlüpfte tapfer in die nicht sonderlich sympathische Rolle eines Alkoholikers, der von seiner düsteren Vergangenheit heimgesucht wird. / Nicholson s'attelle courageusement à ce rôle tout sauf flatteur d'alcoolique hanté par ses mauvaises actions passées.

PAGES 130/131
STILL FROM 'BATMAN' (1989)
Killer Smylex: The Joker (Nicholson) may sell products that put a smile on your face, but their effect is lethal. / Killer-Smylex: Der Joker (Nicholson) verkauft Produkte, die ein Lächeln ins Gesicht zaubern – doch mit tödlichen Folgen. / Risex : Le Joker (Nicholson) vend peut-être des produits qui donnent le sourire, mais leur effet est mortel.

STILL FROM 'BATMAN' (1989)
Jack's advice to Michael Keaton, who plays Batman:
"You've got to let the wardrobe do the acting, kid." /
Nicholson gab Batman-Darsteller Michael Keaton den
Rat: „Junge, du musst das Schauspielen dem Kostüm
überlassen." / Le conseil de Nicholson à Michael
Keaton, qui incarne Batman : « Il faut laisser le costume
jouer pour toi, petit. »

*"The thing I like about the Joker is that his sense
of humor is completely tasteless."*
Jack Nicholson

*„Was mir am Joker am besten gefällt, ist, dass sein
Humor vollkommen geschmacklos ist."*
Jack Nicholson

*« Ce que j'aime chez le Joker, c'est qu'il a un sens
de l'humour du plus parfait mauvais goût. »*
Jack Nicholson

STILL FROM 'BATMAN' (1989)
The Joker says he can't live without the love of Vicki
Vale (Kim Basinger)—but his suicide is just a joke. /
Der Joker behauptet, er könne ohne Vicki Vales (Kim
Basinger) Liebe nicht leben, doch sein Suizidversuch ist
wieder nur ein schlechter Scherz. / Le Joker affirme
qu'il ne peut vivre sans l'amour de Vicki Vale
(Kim Basinger), mais son suicide n'est qu'une farce.

"I was particularly proud of my performance as the Joker. I considered it a piece of pop art."
Jack Nicholson

„Ich war außerordentlich stolz auf meine Darstellung des Jokers. Ich betrachtete es als ein Stück Pop-Art."
Jack Nicholson

« J'étais particulièrement fier de mon interprétation du Joker. Je la considère comme une œuvre de pop art. »
Jack Nicholson

STILL FROM 'BATMAN' (1989)
Jack was paid $6 million for playing The Joker, but his deal included royalties on all Batman merchandise and eventually totaled $60 million. / Nicholson kassierte eine Gage von sechs Millionen Dollar für seine Rolle als Bösewicht „Joker", aber sein Vertrag sicherte ihm eine Gewinnbeteiligung aus dem Verkauf sämtlicher Batman-Artikel zu, sodass er durch den Film letztendlich 60 Millionen US-Dollar verdiente. / Nicholson reçoit 6 millions de dollars pour jouer le Joker, mais son contrat prévoit aussi qu'il touchera des droits sur tous les produits dérivés Batman ; une clause qui lui rapportera 60 millions de dollars en tout.

PAGES 136/137
ON THE SET OF 'THE TWO JAKES' (1990)
Jack fought for years to get this movie made—his pet project, the sequel to *Chinatown*. He eventually directed it himself. / Nicholson kämpfte jahrelang darum, diese Fortsetzung von *Chinatown* drehen zu können, die ihm sehr am Herzen lag. Schließlich übernahm er selbst die Regie. / Nicholson s'est battu pendant des années pour que ce film voie le jour ; cette suite de *Chinatown* est un projet qui lui tient à cœur et il finira par la réaliser lui-même.

STILL FROM 'THE TWO JAKES' (1990)
Jake Gittes (Nicholson) meets Jake Berman (Harvey
Keitel). Can Gittes avoid being corrupted by his dark
double? / Jake Gittes (Nicholson) lernt Jake Berman
(Harvey Keitel) kennen. Kann Gittes verhindern, dass
ihn sein finsterer Doppelgänger korrumpiert? / Jake
Gittes (Nicholson) rencontre Jake Berman (Harvey
Keitel). Gittes se laissera-t-il corrompre par son double
maléfique ?

STILL FROM 'THE TWO JAKES' (1990)
Gittes investigates adultery, murder—and that's just the
beginning of a complicated case that challenges the
viewer's intelligence. / Gittes kommt Ehebruch und
Mord auf die Spur – und das ist nur der Anfang eines
komplizierten Falls, der hohe Ansprüche an die
Intelligenz des Publikums stellt. / Gittes enquête sur un
adultère, un meurtre... et ce n'est que le début d'un cas
difficile qui sollicite toute l'intelligence du spectateur.

STILL FROM 'A FEW GOOD MEN' (1992)
As Marine Colonel Nathan Jessep under interrogation
on the witness stand: "You can't handle the truth!" /
Als Nathan Jessep, Oberst der Marineinfanterie, wird
Nicholson im Zeugenstand verhört: „Sie können die
Wahrheit nicht ertragen!" / Dans le rôle du colonel de la
marine Nathan Jessep, à la barre des témoins : « Vous
voulez la vérité, mais ne pouvez pas la supporter ! »

STILL FROM 'MAN TROUBLE' (1992)
Joan (Ellen Barkin) hires Harry Bliss (Nicholson) to
protect her home against intruders—but he may be one
himself! / Joan (Ellen Barkin) engagiert Harry Bliss
(Nicholson), um ihr Haus gegen Eindringlinge zu
schützen - doch er selbst ist möglicherweise einer von
ihnen! / Joan (Ellen Barkin) engage Harry Bliss
(Nicholson) pour protéger sa maison contre les intrus...
mais peut-être en est-il un lui-même !

STILL FROM 'HOFFA' (1992)
For his performance as union boss Jimmy Hoffa, Jack
was nominated for both best actor (Golden Globes)
and worst actor (Razzies). / Für seine Darstellung
des Gewerkschaftsführers Jimmy Hoffa wurde
Nicholson sowohl als bester (bei den Golden Globes)
als auch als schlechtester (bei den Razzies) Schauspieler
nominiert. / Pour son interprétation du syndicaliste
américain Jimmy Hoffa, Nicholson est à la fois nominé
comme meilleur (Golden Globes) et comme pire
acteur de l'année (Razzies).

ON THE SET OF 'HOFFA' (1992)
Jack got another chance to work with Danny DeVito.
They were boyhood friends in New Jersey, where their
relatives ran a hair salon. / Nicholson hatte erneut die
Möglichkeit, mit Danny DeVito zu arbeiten. Die beiden
waren schon in ihrer Jugend in New Jersey befreundet
gewesen, wo ihre Verwandten einen Friseurladen
betrieben. / Nicholson a l'occasion de retravailler avec
Danny DeVito. Ils ont grandi ensemble dans le New
Jersey, où leurs familles géraient un salon de coiffure.

STILL FROM 'WOLF' (1994)
Alpha male: Randall's appetites include an affair with the boss's daughter (Michelle Pfeiffer). / Alphatier: Auf seinen Raubzügen hat Randall auch eine Affäre mit der Tochter (Michelle Pfeiffer) seines früheren Chefs. / Mâle alpha : les appétits de Randall le poussent à convoiter la fille de son patron (Michelle Pfeiffer).

ARTWORK FOR 'WOLF' (1994)
Mild-mannered publisher Will Randall (Nicholson) is transformed into a sexy beast after being bitten by a wolf. / Nachdem er von einem Wolf gebissen wurde, verwandelt sich der gutmütige Verlagslektor Will Randall (Nicholson) in eine lüsterne Bestie. / Le doux éditeur Will Randall (Nicholson) se change en bête lubrique après avoir été mordu par un loup.

STILL FROM 'THE EVENING STAR' (1996)
She shines longest: Reteamed with Shirley MacLaine
for the sequel to *Terms of Endearment*. / Ein Stern,
der nicht untergeht: Für die Fortsetzung zu *Zeit der
Zärtlichkeit* spielte er erneut an der Seite von Shirley
MacLaine. / Elle brille plus longtemps : nouvelle
collaboration avec Shirley MacLaine pour cette suite
de *Tendres passions*.

STILL FROM 'THE CROSSING GUARD' (1995)
As a disturbed father who seeks vengeance on the
drunk driver who killed his little girl. / Nicholson spielt
einen verwirrten Vater, der sich an dem betrunkenen
Autofahrer rächen will, der seine kleine Tochter auf
dem Gewissen hat. / Un père torturé veut se venger du
chauffard qui a tué sa petite fille.

STILL FROM 'BLOOD AND WINE' (1996)
With partner in crime Victor (Michael Caine, who said
that "Jack restored my heart in doing roles—and my
faith in the business"). / Mit seinem Komplizen Victor
(Michael Caine, der von ihm sagte: „Jack gab mir das
Vertrauen in die Schauspielerei zurück – und in das
Filmgeschäft"). / Avec son partenaire dans le crime,
Victor (Michael Caine, qui a déclaré : « Jack m'a redonné
l'envie du jeu, et ma foi dans ce métier »).

STILL FROM 'BLOOD AND WINE' (1996)
Alex (Nicholson) hopes to start a new life with Cuban
refugee Gabriella (Jennifer Lopez)—but first he must
finance it with a jewel heist! / Alex (Nicholson) möchte
mit dem kubanischen Flüchtlingsmädchen Gabriella
(Jennifer Lopez) ein neues Leben beginnen – das Geld
dazu muss er sich aber erst noch durch einen
Juwelenraub beschaffen! / Alex (Nicholson) espère
démarrer une nouvelle vie avec une réfugiée cubaine,
Gabriella (Jennifer Lopez), mais il ne peut la financer
qu'avec un dernier vol de bijoux !

STILL FROM 'MARS ATTACKS!' (1996)
A female Martian reveals her alien form to President
James Dale (Nicholson) and disturbs his peace of
mind. / Ein Marsweibchen gibt sich Präsident James
Dale (Nicholson) zu erkennen und bringt seinen
Verstand ganz schön durcheinander. / Une Martienne
révèle sa forme extraterrestre au président James Dale
(Nicholson) et bouleverse sa vision du monde.

"Star quality is if you're on stage and a cat walks on and they still watch you."
Jack Nicholson

„Ein Star ist man, wenn man auf der Bühne steht und eine Katze vorbeiläuft und sie immer noch dir zuschauen."
Jack Nicholson

« Une étoffe de star, c'est quand vous êtes sur scène, qu'un chat fait son entrée et que c'est toujours vous qu'on regarde. »
Jack Nicholson

STILL FROM 'MARS ATTACKS!' (1996)
Jack played two parts in this film: a U.S. president and
a cowboy millionaire. / Nicholson spielt in diesem Film
zwei Rollen: den Präsidenten der USA und einen
Cowboy-Millionär. / Nicholson joue deux rôles dans ce
film : un président américain et un cow-boy millionnaire.

STILL FROM 'AS GOOD AS IT GETS' (1997)
"You make me want to be a better man." Misanthropic
Melvin Udall (Nicholson) finds unexpected romance
(with Helen Hunt). / „Deinetwegen möchte ich ein
besserer Mensch sein." Misanthrop Melvin Udall
(Nicholson) findet unerwartet seine große Liebe
(mit Helen Hunt). / « Vous me donnez envie de devenir
meilleur. » Ironie du sort : le misanthrope Melvin Udall
(Nicholson) trouve l'amour (en la personne de
Helen Hunt).

PAGES 154/155
STILL FROM 'AS GOOD AS IT GETS' (1997)
After being forced to care for a gay neighbor's dog,
Melvin grows to love the animal. / Nachdem er
gezwungenermaßen auf den Hund seines schwulen
Nachbarn aufpassen musste, findet Melvin allmählich
Gefallen an dem Tier. / Après avoir été forcé de
s'occuper du chien de son voisin homosexuel, Melvin
en vient à aimer l'animal.

STILL FROM 'THE PLEDGE' (2001)
As a retired cop obsessed with bringing a child
murderer to justice, Jack gives one of his finest
performances. With Robin Wright Penn. / Als
pensionierter Polizist, der besessen ist von dem
Wunsch, einen Kindermörder seiner gerechten Strafe
zuzuführen, liefert Nicholson eine seiner besten
schauspielerischen Leistungen. Mit Robin Wright
Penn. / Flic à la retraite obsédé par l'idée de faire
juger l'assassin d'un enfant, Nicholson offre une de ses
interprétations les plus magistrales. Avec Robin
Wright Penn.

STILL FROM 'THE PLEDGE' (2001)
Jerry Black (Nicholson) follows the clues in a dead girl's drawing to track the man who killed her. / Jerry Black (Nicholson) folgt Spuren in der Zeichnung des toten Mädchens, um ihren Mörder zu finden. / Jerry Black (Nicholson) suit la piste d'un assassin à partir d'un dessin de sa jeune victime.

"He is a very great actor. The bravest, I would say. He has gone from being admired to liked, to appreciated and celebrated, to beloved. He is now beloved."
Director Milos Forman on Jack Nicholson

„Er ist ein ganz großartiger Schauspieler – ich würde sagen, der tüchtigste. Er entwickelte sich von bewundert zu gemocht, zu geschätzt und gefeiert, zu geliebt. Er wird jetzt geliebt."
Regisseur Milos Forman über Jack Nicholson

« C'est un très grand acteur. Le plus courageux, je dirais. Il a été admiré, puis aimé, apprécié et célébré, et enfin adulé. Aujourd'hui, il est adulé. »
Le réalisateur Milos Forman à propos de Jack Nicholson

"Once I'm dead and everyone who knew me dies too, it will be as though I never even existed. What difference has my life made to anyone? None that I can think of."
Warren R. Schmidt (Jack Nicholson), *About Schmidt* **(2002)**

„Wenn ich einmal tot bin und jeder, der mich kannte, auch stirbt, dann wird es sein, als ob ich nie existiert hätte. Welchen Unterschied hat dann mein Leben für irgendjemanden gemacht? Keinen, der mir einfiele."
Warren R. Schmidt (Jack Nicholson), *About Schmidt* **(2002)**

« Quand je serai mort et que tous ceux qui m'ont connu seront morts aussi, ce sera comme si je n'avais jamais existé. Qu'est-ce que ma vie a changé, pour qui ? Je ne vois personne. »
Warren R. Schmidt (Jack Nicholson), *Monsieur Schmidt* **(2002)**

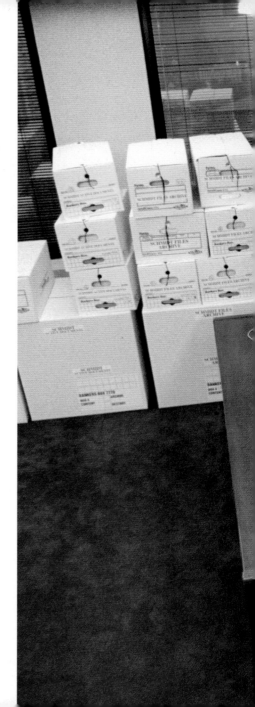

STILL FROM 'ABOUT SCHMIDT' (2002)
Having retired from his job and then lost his wife, Schmidt (Nicholson) wonders whether he has any reason left to live. / Nachdem er pensioniert wurde und seine Frau verloren hat, fragt sich Schmidt (Nicholson), ob sein Leben noch einen Sinn hat. / Monsieur Schmidt (Nicholson) a pris sa retraite puis perdu sa femme : lui reste-t-il une raison de vivre ?

ON THE SET OF 'ABOUT SCHMIDT' (2002)
"You're playing a small man": Director Alexander Payne
instructed Jack to give a quiet, understated
performance. / „Du spielst einen kleinen Mann":
Regisseur Alexander Payne gab Nicholson die
Anweisung, die Rolle still und unauffällig anzulegen. /
« Vous jouez un homme petit » : le réalisateur Alexander
Payne demande à Nicholson de jouer de façon
tranquille et discrète.

*"The only actor more comfortable in front of the
camera than in real life."*
Actor-producer Michael Douglas on Jack Nicholson

*„Der einzige Schauspieler, der sich vor der Kamera
wohler fühlt als im richtigen Leben."*
Schauspieler und Produzent Michael Douglas über
Jack Nicholson

*« Le seul acteur qui soit plus à l'aise devant la
caméra que dans la vraie vie. »*
L'acteur et producteur Michael Douglas à propos de
Jack Nicholson

STILL FROM 'ABOUT SCHMIDT' (2002)
When Schmidt takes to the road in a 35-foot
Winnebago, he finds that life still holds some meaningful
surprises. / Als sich Schmidt in einem zehn Meter langen
Wohnmobil auf die Reise macht, stellt er fest, dass das

Leben noch immer einige Überraschungen für ihn
bereithält. / Quand Schmidt prend la route au volant
d'une Winnebago de dix mètres de long, il découvre que
la vie peut encore lui réserver de drôles de surprises.

"If there's a constant in my work, it is the principle of affirmation. It's the little guy and sometimes he may be moved back, squeezed down by the system, but he tries to creep back up, move forward, affirm his life."
Jack Nicholson

„Wenn es in meinem Leben eine Konstante gibt, dann ist es das Prinzip der Bejahung. Es ist der kleine Mann, und vielleicht erlebt er manchmal Rückschläge, wird vom System nach unten gedrückt, aber er versucht, sich wieder aufzurappeln, nach oben zu kommen, sein Leben zu bejahen."
Jack Nicholson

« S'il y a une constante dans mon travail, c'est le principe d'affirmation. C'est le petit bonhomme qui peut être mis de côté, parfois comprimé par le système, mais qui essaie toujours de remonter à la surface, d'avancer, d'affirmer son existence. »
Jack Nicholson

STILL FROM 'ABOUT SCHMIDT' (2002)
Enjoying the sunshine: As Jack said about Schmidt, "The gradual taking away of things gets him down to his basic essence." / Er genießt die Sonne – Nicholson meinte über Schmidt: „Der allmähliche Verlust von Dingen führt ihn zurück zum eigentlichen Wesen seines Daseins." / Moment de répit sous les doux rayons du soleil. Nicholson a dit de Schmidt : « La disparition progressive de tout ce qu'il a l'oblige à revenir à sa nature profonde. »

STILL FROM 'ANGER MANAGEMENT' (2003)
Psychotic Dr. Buddy Rydell (played by "Wild Man" Jack
Nicholson) seems like the last person to help anyone
with their anger. / Der psychotische Dr. Buddy Rydell
(gespielt vom „Wilden" Jack Nicholson) scheint der
letzte Mensch zu sein, der anderen helfen könnte, ihr
Temperament zu zügeln. / Le psychotique Dr. Buddy
Rydell (Nicholson) semble être la dernière personne au
monde capable d'aider quiconque à maîtriser sa colère.

STILL FROM 'ANGER MANAGEMENT' (2003)
Ironically, timid Dave (Adam Sandler) needs to get
angry—and Dr. Buddy's suing him for a fake neck injury
just might do it. / Ironischerweise muss der ängstliche
Dave (Adam Sandler) lernen, wütend zu werden – und
Dr. Buddy könnte ihn dazu bringen, indem er ihn wegen
einer getürkten Verletzung verklagt. / Le timide Dave
(Adam Sandler), en revanche, aurait besoin de savoir se
mettre en colère, et le fait que le Dr. Buddy le poursuive
en justice pour une fausse blessure à la nuque pourrait
bien l'y aider.

STILLS FROM
'SOMETHING'S GOTTA GIVE' (2003)

Opposite: In a role with some autobiographical truth, Jack plays an ageing playboy who prefers seducing younger women. Above: A heart attack wises him up, and he falls for the mother (Diane Keaton, left) of his latest girlfriend (Amanda Peet). / Links: In einer Rolle, in der ein wenig autobiografische Wahrheit steckt, spielt Nicholson einen alternden Playboy, der es vorzieht, jüngere Frauen zu verführen. Oben: Ein Herzinfarkt bringt ihn zur Vernunft, und er verliebt sich in die Mutter (Diane Keaton, links) seiner letzten Freundin (Amanda Peet). / Page ci-contre: dans un rôle aux accents autobiographiques, Nicholson joue un play-boy vieillissant qui préfère séduire des femmes plus jeunes. Ci-dessus: une crise cardiaque le pousse à s'assagir, et il tombe amoureux de la mère (Diane Keaton, à gauche) de sa dernière petite amie (Amanda Peet).

PAGES 168/169
STILL FROM
'SOMETHING'S GOTTA GIVE' (2003)

Harry (Nicholson) gets Erica (Diane Keaton) to loosen up: "What's with the turtlenecks? It's the middle of summer!" / Harry (Nicholson) bringt Erica (Diane Keaton) dazu, sich etwas lockerer zu geben: „Was soll der Rollkragen? Wir haben Hochsommer!" / Harry (Nicholson) réussit à détendre Erica (Diane Keaton): « C'est quoi, ces cols roulés? On est en plein été!»

STILL FROM 'THE DEPARTED' (2006)
"I smell a rat": Gangster Frank Costello (Nicholson) wonders whether Billy (Leonardo DiCaprio) is a mole within the mob. / „Etwas ist hier faul": Gangster Frank Costello (Nicholson) fragt sich, ob Billy (Leonardo DiCaprio) ein Maulwurf innerhalb der Mafia sein könnte. / « Je sens l'embrouille » : le gangster Frank Costello (Nicholson) se demande si Billy (Leonardo DiCaprio) n'est pas une taupe de la mafia.

ON THE SET OF 'THE DEPARTED' (2006)
Strange that, after all their years and films, this was the first time Jack ever worked with director Martin Scorsese. / Es ist merkwürdig, dass Nicholson nach all den Jahren und all den Filmen hier zum ersten Mal mit Regisseur Martin Scorsese zusammenarbeitete. / Aussi étrange que cela paraisse après tant d'années et de films, Nicholson travaille ici pour la première fois avec le réalisateur Martin Scorsese.

PAGES 172/173
STILL FROM 'THE DEPARTED' (2006)
With Matt Damon. Jack took the part because he was eager to play a wicked villain again. / Mit Matt Damon. Nicholson übernahm die Rolle, weil er unbedingt wieder einmal einen Bösewicht spielen wollte. / Avec Matt Damon. Après plusieurs comédies, Nicholson est très heureux de jouer à nouveau les méchants impitoyables.

*"With my sunglasses on, I'm Jack Nicholson.
Without them, I'm fat and 70."*
Jack Nicholson

*„Mit meiner Sonnenbrille bin ich Jack Nicholson.
Ohne bin ich fett und 70."*
Jack Nicholson

*« Avec mes lunettes de soleil, je suis Jack
Nicholson. Sans elles, je suis gros et j'ai 70 ans. »*
Jack Nicholson

STILL FROM 'THE BUCKET LIST' (2007)
Carter (Morgan Freeman) and Edward (Nicholson) start
out as strangers but end up seeing the world together. /
Anfangs sind sich Carter (Morgan Freeman) und
Edward (Nicholson) fremd, aber am Ende schauen sie
sich gemeinsam die Welt an. / Carter (Morgan Freeman)
et Edward (Nicholson) sont de parfaits étrangers l'un
pour l'autre au départ, mais en viennent à voir le monde
de la même manière.

STILL FROM 'THE BUCKET LIST' (2007)
The two men are terminally ill patients who make a list of things to do before they die. / Die beiden Männer sind todkrank und stellen eine Liste der Dinge auf, die sie vor dem Sterben noch erledigen möchten. / Les deux hommes jouent des malades en phase terminale qui rédigent la liste de ce qu'ils veulent faire avant de mourir.

*"My work motto is: Everything counts.
My life motto is: More good times!"*
Jack Nicholson

*„Mein Arbeitsmotto ist: Alles zählt.
Mein Lebensmotto ist: Mehr Spaß!"*
Jack Nicholson

*« Au travail, ma devise est "Tout compte".
Dans la vie, ma devise est "Plus de bons
moments !" »*
Jack Nicholson

STILL FROM 'THE BUCKET LIST' (2007)
Edward realizes his dream of skydiving: "We live to
die another day." / Edward macht seinen Traum vom
Fallschirmspringen wahr: „Wir leben, um an einem
anderen Tag zu sterben." / Edward réalise son rêve de
saut en parachute : « Nous vivons pour mourir un
autre jour. »

STILL FROM 'THE BUCKET LIST' (2007)
Thanks to his friend Carter, Edward is reunited with his
estranged family and can at last hug his granddaughter. /
Dank seines Freundes Carter findet Edward zu seiner
Familie zurück, von der er sich entfremdet hatte, und
kann endlich seine Enkelin in die Arme schließen. /
Grâce à son ami Carter, Edward retrouve sa famille
et peut enfin serrer sa petite-fille dans ses bras.

PAGE 178
ON THE SET OF 'THE SHINING' (1980)

3
CHRONOLOGY

CHRONOLOGIE
CHRONOLOGIE

CHRONOLOGY

22 April 1937 John Joseph Nicholson Jr. is born. Grows up in Neptune City, New Jersey, believing that his parents are John Joseph Sr. and Ethel May Nicholson (they were actually his grandparents) and that he has an older sister named June (she was actually his mother).

1958 *The Cry Baby Killer* marks Jack's movie debut in the first of several "troubled teen" roles.

1960–1963 Appears in such Roger Corman horror films as *The Little Shop of Horrors*, *The Raven*, and *The Terror*.

1962 Marries Sandra Knight (divorced 1968).

1964–1966 Makes four films with director Monte Hellman, including the existentialist westerns *The Shooting* and *Ride in the Whirlwind*.

1969 Breaks through to stardom in *Easy Rider*. His previous biker films include *The Wild Ride*, *Hells Angels on Wheels*, and *Rebel Rousers*.

1970 Makes his directorial debut with *Drive, He Said*. Later directs *Goin' South* and *The Two Jakes*. Works as an actor for Bob Rafelson for the first time on *Five Easy Pieces*; they subsequently work together on *The King of Marvin Gardens*, *The Postman Always Rings Twice*, *Man Trouble*, and *Blood and Wine*.

1971 Stars in *Carnal Knowledge* for director Mike Nichols, with whom Jack will go on to make *The Fortune*, *Heartburn*, and *Wolf*.

1973 Begins relationship with actress Anjelica Huston, which will last for 17 years.

1975 Makes *The Passenger*, an existentialist road movie, with director Michelangelo Antonioni.

1976 Wins Oscar for best actor for *One Flew Over the Cuckoo's Nest*. Acts with longtime idol Marlon Brando in *The Missouri Breaks*. The fact that Nicholson, Brando, and Warren Beatty are next-door neighbors on Mulholland Drive leads to its being dubbed "Bad Boy Drive."

1980 Makes *The Shining* ("Heeeere's Johnny!") with legendary director Stanley Kubrick.

1984 Wins Oscar for best supporting actor for *Terms of Endearment*. Begins a series of romantic comedies including *Man Trouble*, *As Good as It Gets*, and *Something's Gotta Give*.

1989 Makes $60 million in a lucrative deal for playing the Joker in *Batman*.

1994 Receives Life Achievement Award from the American Film Institute.

1998 Wins another Academy Award for best actor in *As Good as It Gets*.

2002 Gives one of his most subtle performances as a retired insurance man who must find a reason to keep on living in *About Schmidt*.

2003 Plays a therapist in *Anger Management*, poking fun at his own irascible personality. (In 1994, he smashed in a man's car window with a golf club in an incident of road rage.)

2006 Plays a monstrously sadistic gangster in *The Departed* for director Martin Scorsese.

STILL FROM 'THE BORDER' (1982)

CHRONOLOGIE

22. April 1937 John Joseph Nicholson jr. wird geboren. Er wächst in Neptune City (New Jersey) in dem Glauben auf, John Joseph Nicholson sen. und seine Frau Ethel May wären seine Eltern (obwohl sie tatsächlich seine Großeltern waren) und er hätte eine ältere Schwester namens June (die in Wirklichkeit seine Mutter war).

1958 Jack feiert sein Leinwanddebüt in *The Cry Baby Killer*, wo er auch zum ersten Mal die Rolle eines „problembeladenen Teenagers" spielt.

1960–1963 Er tritt in Horrorfilmen von Roger Corman auf, wie zum Beispiel in *Kleiner Laden voller Schrecken*, *Der Rabe: Duell der Zauberer* und *Schloss des Schreckens*.

1962 Er heiratet Sandra Knight (Scheidung 1968).

1964–1966 Er dreht vier Filme unter der Regie von Monte Hellman, darunter die existenzialistischen Western *Das Schießen* und *Ritt im Wirbelwind*.

1969 Er schafft den Durchbruch zum Star mit *Easy Rider*. Davor hatte er unter anderem schon in den Motorradfilmen *The Wild Ride*, *Die wilden Schläger von San Francisco* und *Rebel Riders* mitgewirkt.

1970 Er gibt sein Regiedebüt mit *Drive, He Said*. Später inszeniert er noch *Der Galgenstrick* und *Die Spur führt zurück*. Er schauspielert erstmals unter der Regie von Bob Rafelson in *Ein Mann sucht sich selbst*; die beiden arbeiten erneut zusammen bei *Der König von Marvin Gardens*, *Wenn der Postmann zweimal klingelt*, *Man Trouble* und *Ein tödlicher Cocktail*.

1971 Er spielt eine Hauptrolle in *Die Kunst zu lieben* unter der Regie von Mike Nichols, mit dem er später auch *Mitgiftjäger*, *Sodbrennen* und *Wolf* dreht.

1973 Er beginnt eine Beziehung mit der Schauspielerin Anjelica Huston, die 17 Jahre dauern wird.

**STILL FROM
'SOMETHING'S GOTTA GIVE' (2003)**

1975 Er dreht das existenzialistische Roadmovie *Beruf: Reporter* unter der Regie von Michelangelo Antonioni.

1976 Er wird mit einem Oscar als bester Schauspieler für seine Leistung in *Einer flog über das Kuckucksnest* ausgezeichnet. Er spielt an der Seite seines langjährigen Vorbilds Marlon Brando in *Duell am Missouri*. Die Tatsache, dass Nicholson, Brando und Warren Beatty am Mulholland Drive Nachbarn sind, gibt der Straße den Spitznamen „Bad Boy Drive".

1980 Er dreht *Shining* (mit der berühmten Ed-McMahon-Imitation „Heeeere's Johnny!") unter der Regie des legendären Stanley Kubrick.

1984 Er erhält einen Oscar als bester Nebendarsteller für *Zeit der Zärtlichkeit*. In den folgenden Jahren dreht er eine Reihe von Liebeskomödien, darunter *Man Trouble*, *Besser geht's nicht* und *Was das Herz begehrt*.

1989 Durch einen lukrativen Vertrag erhält er 60 Millionen US-Dollar für seine Rolle als Bösewicht „Joker" in *Batman*.

1994 Er erhält den Life Achievement Award für sein Lebenswerk vom American Film Institute.

1998 Er erhält einen weiteren Academy Award als bester Schauspieler für seine Leistung in *Besser geht's nicht*.

2002 Er liefert in *About Schmidt* eine seiner subtilsten schauspielerischen Leistungen in der Rolle eines pensionierten Versicherungsvertreters, der nach einem Grund für sein Weiterleben sucht.

2003 Indem er einen Psychotherapeuten in *Die Wutprobe: Spürt die Liebe* spielt, macht er sich über seinen eigenen Jähzorn lustig. (Im Jahre 1994 hatte er in einem „Verkehrsanfall" das Autofenster eines anderen Fahrers mit einem Golfschläger zertrümmert.)

2006 Er spielt einen ungeheuer sadistischen Gangster in *Departed: Unter Feinden* unter der Regie von Martin Scorsese.

CHRONOLOGIE

22 avril 1937 Naissance de John Joseph Nicholson Jr. Il grandit à Neptune City (New Jersey), avec ceux qu'il prend pour ses parents, John Joseph Sr. et Ethel May Nicholson (qui sont en fait ses grand-parents), et sa « sœur aînée » June (qui est en vérité sa mère biologique).

1958 *The Cry Baby Killer* marque les débuts de Nicholson sur le grand écran, dans le premier d'une série de rôles d'adolescents « perturbés ».

1960–1963 Apparaît dans trois films d'horreur de Roger Corman : *La Petite Boutique des horreurs*, *Le Corbeau* et *L'Halluciné*.

1962 Épouse Sandra Knight (ils divorceront en 1968).

1964–1966 Tourne quatre films sous la direction de Monte Hellman, parmi lesquels les westerns existentialistes *The Shooting* et *L'Ouragan de la vengeance*.

1969 Accède à la célébrité grâce à *Easy Rider*. Il a déjà tourné plusieurs films de « bikers », notamment *The Wild Ride*, *La Retour des anges de l'enfer* et *Les Motos de la violence*.

1970 Fait ses débuts de réalisateur avec *Vas-y, fonce*. Il réalisera aussi *En route vers le Sud* et *The Two Jakes*. Joue pour la première fois sous la direction de Bob Rafelson, dans *Cinq pièces faciles* ; ils travailleront à nouveau ensemble sur *The King of Marvin Gardens*, *Le facteur sonne toujours deux fois*, *Man Trouble* et *Blood and Wine*.

1971 Premier rôle dans *Ce plaisir qu'on dit charnel* de Mike Nichols, avec lequel il tournera aussi *La Bonne Fortune*, *La Brûlure* et *Wolf*.

1973 Entame avec l'actrice Anjelica Huston une relation qui durera 17 ans.

1975 Tourne *Profession : reporter*, road-movie existentialiste, sous la direction du maître Michelangelo Antonioni.

1976 Remporte l'oscar du Meilleur acteur pour son interprétation dans *Vol au-dessus d'un nid de coucou*. Partage l'affiche avec son idole de longue date, Marlon Brando, dans *Missouri Breaks*. Le tronçon de Mulholland Drive où résident Nicholson, Brando et Warren Beatty est rebaptisé « Bad Boy Drive » (l'avenue des mauvais garçons).

1980 Tourne *Shining* (« Voilà, Johnny ! ») avec le légendaire Stanley Kubrick.

1984 Remporte l'oscar du Meilleur second rôle pour sa prestation dans *Tendres passions*. Se lance dans une série de comédies romantiques, parmi lesquelles *Man Trouble*, *Pour le pire et pour le meilleur* et *Tout peut arriver*.

1989 Empoche un cachet de 60 millions de dollars pour jouer le rôle du Joker dans *Batman*.

1994 Reçoit le Life Achievement Award de l'American Film Institute pour l'ensemble de sa carrière.

1998 Remporte un nouvel oscar du Meilleur acteur pour son interprétation dans *Pour le pire et pour le meilleur*.

2002 Révèle toute l'infinie finesse de son jeu dans le rôle d'un agent d'assurance en retraite qui cherche une raison de continuer à vivre dans *Monsieur Schmidt*.

2003 Joue un thérapeute dans *Self control* où il tourne en dérision sa propre personnalité irascible. (En 1994, rendu fou par la circulation, il avait enfoncé le pare-brise d'un automobiliste avec un club de golf.)

2006 Joue un gangster particulièrement sadique sous la direction de Martin Scorsese dans *Les Infiltrés*.

PORTRAIT (1983)

a Robert Evans production of a

Roman Polanski film

Jack Nicholson · Faye Dunaway

co-starring
JOHN HILLERMAN · PERRY LOPEZ · BURT YOUNG and JOHN HUSTON

production designer   associate producer   music scored by
RICHARD SYLBERT · C.O. ERICKSON · JERRY GOLDSMITH

written by   produced by   directed by
Robert Towne · Robert Evans · Roman Polanski

TECHNICOLOR® · PANAVISION®
A PARAMOUNT PRESENTATION

4

FILMOGRAPHY

FILMOGRAFIE

FILMOGRAPHIE

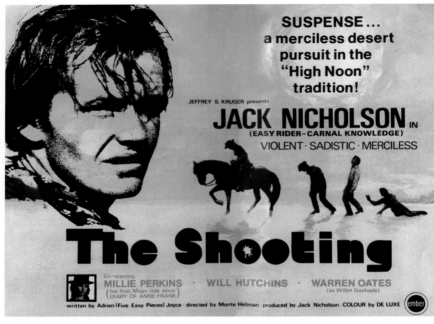

SUSPENSE...
a merciless desert
pursuit in the
"High Noon"
tradition!

JEFFREY S. KRUGER presents

JACK NICHOLSON IN
(EASY RIDER – CARNAL KNOWLEDGE)

VIOLENT · SADISTIC · MERCILESS

The Shooting

Co-starring
MILLIE PERKINS · **WILL HUTCHINS** · **WARREN OATES**
(her first Major role since
DIARY OF ANNE FRANK)   (as Willet Gashade)

written by Adrien (Five Easy Pieces) Joyce · directed by Monte Hellman · produced by Jack Nicholson · COLOUR by DE LUXE   ember

The Cry Baby Killer (1958)
Jimmy Wallace. Director/Regie/réalisation:
Jus Addiss.

The Little Shop of Horrors (dt. *Kleiner Laden voller Schrecken,* **fr.** *La Petite Boutique des horreurs,* **1960)**
Wilbur Force. Director/Regie/réalisation:
Roger Corman.

Too Soon to Love (aka *Teenage Lovers,* **1960)**
Buddy. Director/Regie/réalisation: Richard Rush.

Studs Lonigan (1960)
Weary Reilly. Director/Regie/réalisation: Irving Lerner.

The Wild Ride (aka *Velocity,* **1960)**
Johnny Varron. Director/Regie/réalisation:
Harvey Berman.

The Broken Land (1962)
Will Brocious. Director/Regie/réalisation:
John Bushelman.

The Raven (dt. *Der Rabe: Duell der Zauberer,* **fr.** *Le Corbeau,* **1963)**
Rexford Bedlo. Director/Regie/réalisation:
Roger Corman.

The Terror (dt. *Schloss des Schreckens,* **fr.** *L'Halluciné,* **1963)**
Lieutenant André Duvalier.
Director/Regie/réalisation: Roger Corman.

Thunder Island (1963)
Co-screenwriter/Mitautor des Drehbuchs/
coscénariste: Jack Nicholson.
Director/Regie/réalisation: Jack Leewood.

Ensign Pulver (dt. *Operation Pazifik,* **1964)**
Dolan. Director/Regie/réalisation: Joshua Logan.

Back Door to Hell (1964)
Burnett. Director/Regie/réalisation: Monte Hellman.

Flight to Fury (1964)
Jay Wickham [also screenwriter/auch
Drehbuchautor/également scénariste].
Director/Regie/réalisation: Monte Hellman.

The Shooting (dt. *Das Schießen,* **1965)**
Billy Spear. Director/Regie/réalisation:
Monte Hellman.

Ride in the Whirlwind (dt. *Ritt im Wirbelwind,* **fr.** *L'Ouragan de la vengeance,* **1966)**
Wes [also screenwriter/auch Drehbuchautor/

également scénariste]. Director/Regie/réalisation: Monte Hellman.

Hells Angels on Wheels (dt. *Die wilden Schläger von San Francisco*, fr. *Le Retour des anges de l'enfer*, 1967)
Poet/Dichter/poète. Director/Regie/réalisation: Richard Rush.

Rebel Rousers (dt. *Rebel Riders*, fr. *Les Motos de la violence*, 1967)
Bunny. Director/Regie/réalisation: Martin B. Cohen.

The St. Valentine's Day Massacre (dt. *Chicago-Massaker*, fr. *L'Affaire Al Capone*, 1967)
Gino, the Hit Man/der Berufskiller/le tueur à gages. Director/Regie/réalisation: Roger Corman.

The Trip (1967)
Screenwriter/Drehbuchautor/scénario: Jack Nicholson. Director/Regie/réalisation: Roger Corman.

Psych-Out (1968)
Stoney. Director/Regie/réalisation: Richard Rush.

Head (1968)
Co-screenwriter/Mitautor des Drehbuchs/coscéna-riste: Jack Nicholson. Director/Regie/réalisation: Bob Rafelson.

Easy Rider (1969)
George Hanson. Director/Regie/réalisation: Dennis Hopper.

On a Clear Day You Can See Forever (dt. *Einst kommt der Tag*, fr. *Melinda*, 1970)
Tad Pringle. Director/Regie/réalisation: Vincente Minnelli.

Five Easy Pieces (dt. *Ein Mann sucht sich selbst*, fr. *Cinq pièces faciles*, 1970)
Robert Eroica Dupea. Director/Regie/réalisation: Bob Rafelson.

Drive, He Said (fr. *Vas-y, fonce*, 1971)
Screenwriter, director/Drehbuch und Regie/scénario et réalisation: Jack Nicholson.

Carnal Knowledge (dt. *Die Kunst zu lieben*, fr. *Ce plaisir qu'on dit charnel*, 1971)
Jonathan Fuerst. Director/Regie/réalisation: Mike Nichols.

A Safe Place (dt. *Ein Zauberer an meiner Seite*, fr. *Un coin tranquille*, 1971)
Mitch. Director/Regie/réalisation: Henry Jaglom.

The King of Marvin Gardens (dt. *Der König von Marvin Gardens*, 1972)

David Staebler. Director/Regie/réalisation: Bob Rafelson.

The Last Detail (dt. *Das letzte Kommando*, fr. *La Dernière Corvée*, 1973)
Billy "Bad Ass" Buddusky. Director/Regie/réalisation: Hal Ashby.

Chinatown (1974)
J. J. "Jake" Gittes. Director/Regie/réalisation: Roman Polanski.

Professione: reporter (eng. *The Passenger*, dt. *Beruf: Reporter*, fr. *Profession: reporter*, 1975)
David Locke. Director/Regie/réalisation: Michelangelo Antonioni.

Tommy (1975)
The Specialist/Der Spezialist/l'expert. Director/Regie/réalisation: Ken Russell.

The Fortune (dt. *Mitgiftjäger*, fr. *La Bonne Fortune*, 1975)
Oscar Sullivan (aka/alias Oscar Dix). Director/Regie/réalisation: Mike Nichols.

One Flew Over the Cuckoo's Nest (dt. *Einer flog über das Kuckucksnest*, fr. *Vol au-dessus d'un nid de coucou*, 1975)
Randle Patrick McMurphy. Director/Regie/réalisation: Milos Forman.

The Missouri Breaks (dt. *Duell am Missouri*, fr. *Missouri Breaks*, 1976)
Tom Logan. Director/Regie/réalisation: Arthur Penn.

The Last Tycoon (dt. *Der letzte Tycoon*, fr. *Le Dernier Nabab*, 1976)
Brimmer. Director/Regie/réalisation: Elia Kazan.

Goin' South (dt. *Der Galgenstrick*, fr. *En route vers le Sud*, 1978)
Henry Lloyd Moon. Director/Regie/réalisation: Jack Nicholson.

The Shining (dt. *Shining*, fr. *Shining*, 1980)
Jack Torrance. Director/Regie/réalisation: Stanley Kubrick.

The Postman Always Rings Twice (dt. *Wenn der Postmann zweimal klingelt*, fr. *Le facteur sonne toujours deux fois*, 1981)
Frank Chambers. Director/Regie/réalisation: Bob Rafelson.

Ragtime (1981)
Pirate at beach/Pirat am Strand/un pirate sur la plage. Director/Regie/réalisation: Milos Forman.

Reds (1981)
Eugene O'Neill. Director/Regie/réalisation: Warren Beatty.

The Border (dt. *Grenzpatrouille*, fr. *Police frontière*, 1982)
Charlie Smith. Director/Regie/réalisation: Tony Richardson.

Terms of Endearment (dt. *Zeit der Zärtlichkeit*, fr. *Tendres passions*, 1983)
Garrett Breedlove. Director/Regie/réalisation: James L. Brooks.

Prizzi's Honor (dt. *Die Ehre der Prizzis*, fr. *L'Honneur des Prizzi*, 1985)
Charley Partanna. Director/Regie/réalisation: John Huston.

Heartburn (dt. *Sodbrennen*, fr. *La Brûlure*, 1986)
Mark Forman. Director/Regie/réalisation: Mike Nichols.

The Witches of Eastwick (dt. *Die Hexen von Eastwick*, fr. *Les Sorcières d'Eastwick*, 1987)
Daryl Van Horne. Director/Regie/réalisation: George Miller.

Broadcast News (dt. *Nachrichtenfieber*, 1987)
Bill Rorich, the Anchorman/der Nachrichtensprecher/présentateur. Director/Regie/réalisation: James L. Brooks.

Ironweed (dt. *Wolfsmilch*, fr. *La Force du destin*, 1987)
Francis Phelan. Director/Regie/réalisation: Hector Babenco.

Batman (1989)
The Joker/der Joker/le Joker (aka/alias Jack Napier). Director/Regie/réalisation: Tim Burton.

The Two Jakes (dt. *Die Spur führt zurück*, fr. alias *Piège pour un privé*, 1990)
J. J. "Jake" Gittes. Director/Regie/réalisation: Jack Nicholson.

Man Trouble (1992)
Eugene Earl Axline (aka/alias Harry Bliss). Director/Regie/réalisation: Bob Rafelson.

A Few Good Men (dt. *Eine Frage der Ehre*, fr. *Des hommes d'honneur*, 1992)
Colonel Nathan R. Jessep. Director/Regie/réalisation: Rob Reiner.

Hoffa (dt. *Jimmy Hoffa*, 1992)
James R. "Jimmy" Hoffa. Director/Regie/réalisation: Danny DeVito.

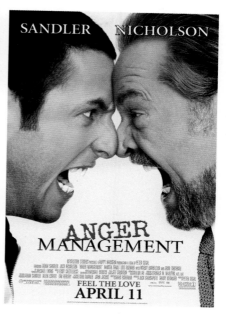

Wolf (1994)
Will Randall. Director/Regie/réalisation:
Mike Nichols.

The Crossing Guard (fr. *Crossing Guard*, 1995)
Freddy Gale. Director/Regie/réalisation:
Sean Penn.

The Evening Star (dt. *Jahre der Zärtlichkeit*, fr. *Étoile du soir*, 1996)
Garrett Breedlove. Director/Regie/réalisation:
Robert Harling.

Blood and Wine (dt. *Ein tödlicher Cocktail*, 1996)
Alex Gates. Director/Regie/réalisation:
Bob Rafelson.

Mars Attacks! (1996)
President/Präsident/le président James Dale
& Art Land. Director/Regie/réalisation:
Tim Burton.

As Good as It Gets (dt. *Besser geht's nicht*, fr. *Pour le pire et pour le meilleur*, 1997)
Melvin Udall. Director/Regie/réalisation:
James L. Brooks.

The Pledge (dt. *Das Versprechen*, 2001)
Jerry Black. Director/Regie/réalisation: Sean Penn.

About Schmidt (fr. *Monsieur Schmidt*, 2002)
Warren R. Schmidt. Director/Regie/réalisation:
Alexander Payne.

Anger Management (dt. *Die Wutprobe: Spürt die Liebe*, fr. *Self control*, 2003)
Dr. Buddy Rydell. Director/Regie/réalisation:
Peter Segal.

Something's Gotta Give (dt. *Was das Herz begehrt*, fr. *Tout peut arriver*, 2003)
Harry Sanborn. Director/Regie/réalisation:
Nancy Meyers.

The Departed (dt. *Departed: Unter Feinden*, fr. *Les Infiltrés*, 2006)
Frank Costello. Director/Regie/réalisation:
Martin Scorsese.

The Bucket List (dt. *Das Beste kommt zum Schluss*, fr. *Sans plus attendre*, 2007)
Edward Cole. Director/Regie/réalisation:
Rob Reiner.

BIBLIOGRAPHY

Baratta, Tommy: *Cooking for Jack.* New York, 1996.
Bingham, Dennis: *Acting Male: Masculinities in the Films of James Stewart, Jack Nicholson, and Clint Eastwood.* New Brunswick, N.J., 1994.
Braithwaite, Bruce: *The Films of Jack Nicholson.* St. Paul, Minn., 1978.
Brode, Douglas: *The Films of Jack Nicholson.* Secaucus, N.J., 1996.
Brottman, Mikita (Ed.): *Jack Nicholson: Movie Top Ten.* London, 1999.
Campbell, Nancy: *Jack Nicholson.* New York, 1994.
Crane, Robert David and Christopher Fryer: *Jack Nicholson, Face to Face.* New York, 1975.
Dickens, Norman: *Jack Nicholson: The Search for a Superstar.* New York, 1975.
Didier, Jack: *Jack Nicholson.* Paris, 1981.
Douglas, Edward: *Jack: The Great Seducer: The Life and Many Loves of Jack Nicholson.* New York, 2004.
Downing, David: *Jack Nicholson: A Biography.* New York, 1984.
Durant, Philippe: *Jack Nicholson.* Clamart, 1990.
Eaton, Michael: *Chinatown.* London, 1997.
Heinzlmeier, Adolf: *Jack Nicholson: Hollywoods Wolf im Schafspelz.* Bergisch Gladbach, 1991.
Hill, Lee: *Easy Rider.* London, 1996.
Horvitz, Louis J.: *The American Film Institute Salute to Jack Nicholson.* Republic Entertainment, 1994 (videotape).

McDougal, Dennis: *Five Easy Decades: How Jack Nicholson Became the Biggest Movie Star in Modern Times.* Hoboken, N.J., 2008.
McGilligan, Patrick: *Jack's Life: A Biography of Jack Nicholson.* London, 1995.
Parker, John: *Jack: The Biography of Jack Nicholson.* London, 2007.
Schiach, Don: *Jack Nicholson: The Complete Film Guide.* London, 1999.
Schneider, Wolf: *Jack Nicholson Tribute Book: American Film Institute Life Achievement Award.* Los Angeles, 1994.
Shepherd, Donald: *Jack Nicholson: An Unauthorized Biography.* New York, 1991.
Siegel, Barbara and Scott Siegel: *Jack Nicholson: The Unauthorized Biography.* New York, 1991.
Sylvester, Derek: *Jack Nicholson.* London, New York, 1982.
Thompson, Peter: *Jack Nicholson: The Life and Times of an Actor on the Edge.* Secaucus, N.J., 1997.
Zurhorst, Meinolf and Lothar R. Just: *Jack Nicholson: Seine Filme, sein Leben.* Munich, 1983.

Websites
www.imdb.com
www.jacknicholson.org
www.jack-nicholson.info

IMPRINT

© 2009 TASCHEN GmbH
Hohenzollernring 53, D-50672 Köln
www.taschen.com

Editor/Picture Research: Paul Duncan/Wordsmith Solutions
Editorial Coordination: Martin Holz, Cologne
Production Coordination: Nadia Najm, Cologne
German Translation: Thomas J. Kinne, Nauheim
French Translation: Alice Pétillot, Paris
Multilingual Production: www.arnaudbriand.com, Paris
Typeface Design: Sense/Net, Andy Disl and Birgit Eichwede, Cologne

Printed in China
ISBN 978-3-8365-0853-7

To stay informed about upcoming TASCHEN titles, please request our magazine at www.taschen.com/magazine or write to TASCHEN, Hohenzollernring 53, D-50672 Cologne, Germany, contact@taschen.com, Fax: +49-221-254919. We will be happy to send you a free copy of our magazine which is filled with information about all of our books.